Offensive Game and Practice Planning for Winning Football

Steve Axman

ISBN: 978-1-60679-201-8
Library of Congress Control Number: 2011945693
Cover design: Studio J Art & Design
Book layout: Studio J Art & Design
Front cover photo: ©Charles Baus/Cal Sport Media/ZUMAPRESS.com
Diagrams: Brenden Murphy

Coaches Choice
P.O. Box 1828
Monterey, CA 93942
www.coacheschoice.com

Dedication

To a wonderful person and a wonderful mother—Margaret Axman

Acknowledgments

With any acknowledgment, I seem to always have to start with my two greatest mentors, Homer Smith and Larry Smith. I also learned a lot from Mouse Davis concerning game planning and play calling. In addition, Keith Gilbertson had a big impact on me with regard to game-plan design and play calling. I have also had some great help from many of the fine coaches I have had the pleasure of working with, such as Brent Myers, Charlie Dickey, Willie Peete, Lindy Infante, Mark Lunsford, Bruce Tarbox, Mike Mikolayunas, Gary Moeller, Gary Bernardi, Ted Williams, Jack Elway, June Jones, Dave Baldwin, Steve Kragthorpe, Ken Zampese, Eric Price, Marty Mornhinweg, Rob Phenicie, Jonathan Smith, Dan Finn, Jeremy Theilbahr, and Luther Carr.

Thanks also go to Shelly MacLam, Kim Axman, and Marie Axman for helping develop parts of this manuscript.

Contents

Introduction

It's 11:30 a.m. on a fall, Sunday morning. You just played a tough, conference game yesterday which, hopefully, you won. You just finished breakfast and are combing through the local newspaper's sport section, reading about yesterday's game results with that last cup of coffee in your hand. On the other hand, perhaps, you are just finishing attending church services with your family or giving yourself a much needed reward of sleeping in until the last possible moment.

Now, however, you have a 15-minute drive to the office because "... it's time to go back to work." Whether you won or lost yesterday (and, of course, winning makes it so much more joyful and motivating to get back to your desk), a new weekly opponent awaits you a mere 145 hours from now. That particular number of hours might vary from program to program or schedule to schedule. You might be a high school coach, and it is Saturday morning after having played a Friday night game. As a result, you have a Saturday morning work reporting time of 9:00 a.m. (or 8:00 a.m. or 10:00 a.m.) in your effort to prepare for next Friday night's 7:00 p.m. kick-off.

No matter what your weekly, or seasonal, timeframe schedule , the bottom line is that a coach only has a set, specific amount of time to prepare for his next week's upcoming opponent. A coach only has a specific number of hours to devise a sound and, hopefully, effective game plan to help secure another possible victory. Furthermore, within that total work load hourly timeframe, the coach must, just as importantly, develop effective weekly, and daily, practice plans. These plans must provide the coach with the opportunity to maximize his team's efforts to practice that specific, weekly game plan.

Adherence to three key concepts is essential when developing a weekly game plan—organization, time management, and coordination. Collectively, they are the building blocks of both an effective offensive game and an effective practice plan. They serve as the underlying roadmap to ensure that a team is at its very best come kick-off time, be it Friday night at 7:00 p.m. or Saturday afternoon at 1:00 p.m.

Offensive Game and Practice Planning for Winning Football was written to help coaches to efficiently and effectively work with the precious, but definitely limited, amount of hours they have at their disposal within the course of a game week. The book presents effective concepts and strategies that can help coaches put together a high-scoring offensive game plan, as well as devise a practice plan that can best help prepare their offensive players to face whatever defensive efforts their upcoming opponent will employ to try to stop them.

More likely than not, some coaches (particularly high school coaches) may feel that the information presented in this book does not apply to them. "You're a college coach," they might state. "You have all day to game plan and to get ready to have a well-organized practice. I'm also a math (or science, English, or social studies) teacher. I have to teach classes. I have to grade tests!"

While this situation may very well be true, they and their team's offense still have to be ready to face an opponent who may jump into a Bear, double eagle defense on third and short or into a stack defense on the goal line. As such, their game plan must be ready to make play calls in whatever specific situations may occur. Accordingly, their team's offense must be well-practiced and prepared to handle particular game-day problems and challenges as they arise. Given the common scenario where high school coaches have even less preparation time than their collegiate counterparts, the key concepts of organization, time management, and practice planning coordination become all the more important.

In reality, a coach should not simply try to rationalize a loss or a poor seasonal record on lack of time to properly put together an effective game and practice plan. Rather, he must efficiently and effectively utilize whatever time he does have. Without question, managing his preparation time properly is the best step he can take to prepare his offense to help his team be victorious.

It is important to note that while *Offensive Game and Practice Planning for Winning Football* deals with *offensive* game planning and *offensive* practice planning, the vast majority of the concepts presented in this book can easily be flipped around and applied effectively by a defensive staff. For example, a team's defensive staff has to have its defenders ready to make the appropriate third-and-short defensive call against the power I offense that its opponent typically employs in such a third-and-short or fourth-and-short situation. Similar to the response required on the offensive side of the ball, once a defensive staff decides on a particular defensive front and secondary call that should be made in specific (e.g., third- or fourth-and-short) situations, it must then make sure that the defensive players have the sufficient amount of quality, targeted practice time to be properly prepared to execute as planned. Being properly prepared allows them to be effective in such situations come game time.

Special teams coaches can also borrow from the concepts detailed in this book to help elicit sound special teams play once the ball is kicked off. Whatever phase of the game is involved (offense, defense, special teams), the key words and concepts are all the same—organization, time management, and coordination. Individually and collectively, each is important if a coach is to be able to get the most of his team's limited game week preparation time.

Given that I am a college coach, this book employs a weekly game time block in which the previous week's game was on Saturday afternoon and the upcoming week's game is also scheduled for a Saturday afternoon. On the other hand, kickoff times can vary from league to league and competitive level to competitive level. Accordingly, the time blocks may need to be adjusted to a team's specific weekly game-preparation schedule. Such a calendar of events might be consistent for a team's entire fall seasonal schedule, or it may become necessary to make adjustments for a unique happening, for example, a night game or a season-ending Thanksgiving day game with a noon kickoff time.

Increasingly, television is another factor that can disrupt the amount of time that coaches have to devote to their game plan and practice plan preparation. For example, a local area's television station may suddenly award a local high school the honor of playing in the station's "Thursday Night Game of the Week." When that occurs, both teams are confronted by a situation where they have a full day or two less to game plan and practice. Fortunately, both teams are probably facing the same set of circumstances.

On occasion, college teams encounter the same game-day or game-time change situation. Even the pros are not totally immune to such problems, although they usually have a set seasonal game-day and time schedule.

One way or the other—high school or college—the critical issue is the same. How do coaches organize and utilize the limited time they have to devise an effective game plan and to properly plan their practices so that their players are well-prepared come game time? *Offensive Game and Practice Planning for Winning Football* offers a resource that can help coaches use whatever time they have available to effectively and efficiently game and practice plan so that their teams are well-prepared and ready to compete at kickoff.

> There are two words that I *never* allow
> my assistant coaches to use:
> " … that's easy!"
> NOTHING in football coaching IS EASY!

1

Game and Practice Planning Begins in the Off-Season

As was discussed in the introduction, a coach may very well find himself in a situation where it's 11:30 a.m. on a Sunday morning, the day after his team has just played a game. He's getting into the car to drive to the office to start work for next week's game preparation at 12:00 noon. Why 12:00 noon? Why not 1:00 p.m.? ... or 3:00 p.m.? Hey it's Sunday! Being Sunday, he may feel that he should not work at all. At Brigham Young University, my good friend head coach Bronco Mendenhall doesn't have his staff work on Sunday. Sunday, for his staff, is a day for religious worship and for spending time with family. Bronco's approach has not held the BYU program back, given that the Cougars' football program is obviously of championship caliber.

The key point to remember is that with regard to how coaches spend their preparation time, they have a number of viable options. Whether a staff starts its new game work week on a Sunday morning (or Saturday morning after a Friday night game) at 8:00 a.m., 1 p.m., or doesn't work on Sunday at all is not the primary factor of concern. What is key is that a coach's new game work-week's starting time and actual game work-week structure should have been established long ago in the off-season. An assistant coach shouldn't have to ask his head coach "... what time are we in tomorrow?" A staff shouldn't have to address the frustration of dealing with a situation involving one or two of the team's assistant coaches straggling into work seemingly late because they were never told, or they never found out, exactly what time the head coach wanted everyone to be in the office the next day. Proper off- or pre-season organization and planning should have taken care of that potential issue long ago. The same is true for Mondays and Tuesdays and every other day of a game work week.

Set a Weekly Game-Week Timeframe Work Schedule

When staff members know they are to be at work consistently at 12:00 noon on a Sunday, all coaches can plan to use those few unscheduled, precious Sunday morning hours personally in whatever way they want, for example, going to church services with their family, having a big breakfast at home or at a local restaurant, or just sleeping in late. Most importantly, the coaches who don't have to "report to duty" until noon would be aware of the fact that the scheduled short block of time would consistently be theirs to use as they please, whether it be to provide themselves with a dead-time break to recharge their batteries or to spend time with their families.

The key to be noted is that the head coach and/or coaching staff should develop a weekly game-week time schedule that effectively works around the timeframe needs of that particular staff in their particular game-day/weekly framework. Depending on the competitive level, it is essential that the outside demands on the time of the staff be considered in whatever schedule is devised. For example, it would be counterproductive to set a 10:00 to 11:30 a.m. preparation work-plan block of time on a Tuesday to address blitz pick-up planning if the majority of the staff would be teaching their high school classes at that time. An underlying objective of this book is to provide coaches with suggestions concerning how to make the best utilization of the limited amount of time that they have available to develop an effective offensive game plan. Another basic goal of this book is to detail what coaches can do to successfully lay out the best way to efficiently practice the game plan during the game week's preparation for the upcoming contest.

As discussed previously, the weekly, in-season work-time schedule should be well-established beforehand and made known to the staff well before the first game of the season for the team. It is important to remember that circumstances may dictate a need for flexibility in the schedule. If 12:00 noon on Sundays is established as the staff's reporting time, then an assistant coach can plan to attend church services if he, and his family, wants to do so. On the other hand, an assistant coach may ask, "Hey coach, our church's service is at 11:00. Can we come in at 1:00?" Why not? If the head coach's goal is to work on Sundays for eight hours, why not push the schedule forward by an hour to accommodate a staff member's wishes and needs, if at all possible. In this instance, the staff would just have to work an hour later than the head coach had initially planned. Another example might be to have the staff come in at 9:00 a.m., take an hour's lunch break, and then go home at 7:00 p.m. to a slightly later family dinner at home, a schedule that enables the staff to get in the desired nine hours of work on a Sunday.

Truth be known, nothing is wrong with the latter schedule either. The key factor is for the head coach to decide the Sunday work-day time length and then adjust it as appropriate. Within the context of the preparation in our society of Sunday as a day of rest, the day after a game can, sometimes, be one of the only days in a game week that a coach can be afforded a few hours of rest, leisure, and/or family time.

When I was a head coach, I liked having the wives bring in a potluck dinner dish to be shared by everyone at the office for a 5:00 to 6:00 p.m. Sunday staff dinner together. In actuality, we cut out the half hour of travel time to go home for dinner, while providing our staff with the opportunity to have an enjoyable hour's dinner with all of the families as a group. We were even careful to have each wife be assigned an "adopted" single coach to feed, so that every staff member could partake in the healthy family atmosphere that we were trying to create. Everyone has to eat anyway, so why not schedule such a Sunday night staff family dinner for an hour or so. Not only can the event help relieve the stress that is often associated with the long work hours of coaching football, it can also provide some much-needed additional family time.

One old adage can be especially true for the coaching wife. "If momma's not happy, no one's happy." Activities such as a one-hour weekly, social potluck dinner for the staff and families, be it Sunday night or any night of the week during the season, can greatly help to make momma, the kids, and the coaches happy or, at a minimum ... happier. In addition, an event that precludes staff members from having to drive home might actually conserve a little bit more of that precious, small amount of time that has previously been discussed. Without question, every bit of work time devoted to getting a weekly game plan ready and to preparing to practice that game plan enhances the likelihood of a game-week ending victory, which would make everyone happy.

Figure 1-1 illustrates an example of a weekly, in-season staff work schedule. Over the years, I have seen this particular schedule work very well in a number of instances.

Coaches should keep in mind that quantity does not necessarily mean quality when it comes to successfully managing the time available for game and practice planning. If a staff knows it will have "x" number of hours to utilize on a weekly basis to get an effective offensive game plan put together and to properly plan for their team's practice needs, they will almost always find a way to make those limited, condensed number of hours work. The biggest problem that occurs during the course of weekly offensive game and practice plan preparation is usually not a lack of time, rather, it's often the inefficient, wasteful use of the time that a coach may actually have available.

At this point, a coach might ask, "... why are the subjects of "when to report every day" and "when to take lunch and dinner breaks" in a book about offensive game and practice planning?" The reason is very straightforward. Without an in-season, game-week organizational time framework that the entire staff can work from, an offensive (or defensive or special teams) staff cannot appropriately organize its own time schedule and efforts. Another point of possible contention might be "... an hour and a half lunch break? ... time to work out? Who's kidding whom? We can barely get out of the staff room in time to get on the practice field. ... Come on, coach. We can't go home at 9:00 o'clock. We have too much to do!"

Even though the aforementioned example is based on the timeframe that I have employed in my career as a college coach, coaches usually dictate their own

Sunday	
12:00-5:00	Staff
6:00-7:00	Dinner
7:00-9:00	Staff
Monday/Tuesday/Wednesday	
7:00-12:00	Staff
12:00-1:30	Lunch/Workout/Personal
1:30-6:00	Staff
6:00-7:00	Dinner
7:00-9:00	Staff
Thursday	
8:00-12:00	Staff
12:00-1:30	Lunch/Workout/Personal
1:30-6:00	Staff
6:00	Off
Friday	
8:00-1:00	Off/Personal
1:00-6:00	Staff
6:00-7:00	Team Dinner
7:00-7:30	Special Teams Meeting
7:30-8:30	Offensive/Defensive Unit Meetings
8:30-9:00	Final Game Procedure Meetings With Head Coach
Saturday	
9:30-11:00	Staff
11:00-6:00	Game-Day Procedures
6:00	Off

Figure 1-1. Staff weekly in-season work schedule

time management schedule, regardless of their team's level of competition. It is also important to keep in mind that several other factors can affect the efforts involved in setting and managing an overall weekly game-week timeframe schedule.

The time when a staff is released at the end of the day is one example of a factor that can affect a time management schedule. For example, the sample schedule shows a consistent 9:00 p.m. "go home" timeframe. "Coach, we have to at least go to 10:00 p.m. … or 11:00 … or 12:00." In reality, I have worked on staffs that have stayed in the office until even 1:00 or 2:00 a.m. For some head coaches, coordinators, and staff, such late work hours serve as a badge of tough, "macho" coaching. Over many years of coaching, I have seen two things occur when such long, late work hours are the rule of thumb—unproductive work and tired coaches. More often than not, when we toiled until 1:30 a.m., our normal reaction the next morning after we had an opportunity to review what we planned during those late hours the previous evening was, "… what were we thinking?"

As a rule, tired minds do not work well. As such, late-hour work is usually very unproductive or, even, counterproductive. It can actually be a time-waster. It can also help generate tired, mistake-prone coaches.

Consistently using a timeframe schedule that allows a staff to go home at a decent time every night (e.g., 9:00 p.m., 10:00 p.m.) enhances the likelihood that the coaches will be fresh—physically, as well as mentally. All factors considered, fresh coaches usually think and work better. The enhanced clarity and efficiency of such thinking can impact more than the next day or two. It can also have an affect on the overall season as well. Although a staff can push through August, September, and October working late "burning the midnight oil," sooner, or later, such toil *will* take its toll.

Unfortunately, late work hours may take their toll at the worst time come November when, hopefully, a team is in the midst of a title-seeking championship battle. Without question, at such a point in its season, with a team facing its most competitive challenges, a team would much rather have a relatively fresh, rested, and ready-to-go group of coaches on its staff, rather than an assortment of individuals who are exhausted and fast approaching end-of-season burn-out.

To some individuals, providing a lunch hour (or hour and a half) to give staff members time to work out may also seem to be a luxury that a team (especially on the high school level) may not be able to afford. In reality, a 40-minute period lunch break may not provide enough time to change into workout gear, work out, shower, and then switch back into civilian clothes again. On the other hand, just like providing a timeframe schedule that allows coaches to get the proper amount of sleep and rest, scheduling specific time for coaches to exercise can do a lot to help produce alert coaches who remain fresh all season long.

Most coaches tell their players that in order to be in the best possible condition that they need proper exercise, rest, and nutrition. A coaching staff during a season is really no different. While working out during the school-day lunch period may not be accommodating enough, setting a coaches' workout time (e.g., for a half hour as soon as the coaches and players leave the practice field) may be just the prescription for health that a staff needs. One somewhat high-profile example of such an option in action is a high school staff that meets, as a group, for 45 minutes before the school day starts to work out together in a motivating, enjoyable manner.

As such, coaches should check their timeframe schedule. After carefully examining this schedule, they often will discover time to not only develop exceptional game-day offensive plans and effective practice plans, but a fresh, well-rested, alert coaching staff as well. As stated previously, the prime focus in this regard must be on quality, rather than quantity. No one questions the fact that coaching during the actual season can be long, grueling, and arduous. In that regard, adhering to proper time-management principles can greatly help to eliminate wasted, unfocused time, as well as help ensure maximal work efforts by sharp, alert coaches.

Fit Daily Game and Practice Plan Needs Into the Weekly Game Week Timeframe Work Schedule

Once the head coach has established the weekly, in-season, game-week timeframe work schedule, it is then the job of the offensive coordinator to develop daily work schedules that adequately address the team's game and practice planning needs. The first step that the offensive coordinator needs to take is to block out whatever time the head coach deems necessary for total organizational, offensive, defensive, and kicking-game staff meetings. A staff may report to work at 7:00 a.m. on Mondays, Tuesdays, and Wednesdays. The head coach, however, may want to have half hour daily meeting for the entire football staff at 7:00 a.m., as soon as the staff reports. On the other hand, the head coach might want the meeting to be set for 45 minutes starting at 9:30 a.m. Then again, the head coach may want to have a practice plan coordinator meeting on practice days to be sure the offense, defense, and special teams practice needs are well-coordinated, with regard to such factors as offensive-defensive practice interaction, practice field usage, and equipment needs. One way or the other, the offensive coordinator needs to plan his offensive daily game and practice plan needs around the schedule of the head coach's full staff meeting needs.

Figure 1-2 illustrates an example of a weekly day-by-day game and practice plan schedule that an offensive staff could consistently utilize. The key word in the aforementioned sentence is "could." This example shows the type of schedule that I would use. Why? … because it fits *my* needs as an offensive coordinator and the needs of *my* staff as I incorporate our team's game and practice planning needs into a weekly, day-by-day plan schedule, according to the timeframe and hours with which I have to work. On the other hand, the weekly day-by-day game and practice plan scheduling of other coaches must fit *their* weekly and daily timeframe and the hours that are available to them. In reality, the weekly and daily timeframe schedule of a high school might vary a lot from the example in Figure 1-2 if their schedule needs to be worked around a Friday night seasonal game schedule, rather than a Saturday afternoon seasonal game schedule, as I do. As stated previously, the key factor for a coach is to examine his weekly schedule to see what hours he has, on a weekly and daily basis, to accommodate his team's game and practicing plan needs.

Sunday	Monday	Tuesday	Wednesday	Thursday	Friday	Saturday
	7:00 – Staff meet	7:00 – Staff meet	7:00 – Staff meet	8:00 – Staff meet	Travel schedule (home schedule see 1:00 pm onward)	
	7:30 – Game plan: base, par down offense, and second and long offense	7:30 – Plan and script practice	7:30 – Finish red zone game plan	8:30 – Game plan: coming-out offense, slow-four minute, slow-minute, hurry-hurry offense		9:30 – Walkthrough session
			10:00 – Plan and script practice	10:30 – Plan and script practice		10:00 – Team breakfast
						11:00 – Pre-game procedures
12:00 – Grade previous day's game video	12:00 – Lunch	12:00 – Lunch	12:00 – Lunch	12:00 – Lunch		
	1:30 – Game plan	1:30 – Staff meet	1:30 – Staff meet	1:30 – Staff meet	1:00 – Staff meet	1:00 – Kickoff
2:00 – Offensive staff review previous day's game		2:00 – Unit/ positional meetings with players	2:00 – Unit/ positional meetings with players	2:00 – Unit/ positional meetings with players	2:00 – Unit/ positional meetings with players	
3:00 – Offensive staff review game with head coach		3:00 – Practice	3:00 – Practice	3:00 – Practice	3:00 – Practice	
4:30 – Review previous day's game with players	4:30 – Light team practice (contition)					
6:00 – Dinner	6:00 – Dinner	6:00 – Dinner	6:00 – Dinner	6:00 – Depart	6:00 – Team dinner	6:00 – Depart
7:00 – Review new opponent video as staff	7:00 – Game plan: third down offense	7:00 – Review practice video	7:00 – Review practice video		7:30 – Unit meetings with players	
8:45 – Initial thoughts		8:15 – Game plan: red zone	8:15 – Recruit calls		8:00 – Head coach meeting	
9:00 – Depart	9:00 – Depart	9:00 – Depart	9:00 – Depart		9:00 – Depart	

Figure 1-2. Weekly day-by-day offensive practice plan schedule model

Flexibility Needs

Within the context of a weekly, day-by-day game and practice plan schedule, a good deal of flexibility must be maintained. One of the best features of such a schedule is that it forces a coach to plan completely for all facets of a football game. That approach encompasses being prepared for the many unique situations that might occur during the course of the game. For example, the opposition's punt is downed on a team's own six-inch line. No problem. The receiving team's coach has already set a response in motion with his team's coming-out offense plan, which it practiced two days ago. That plan might entail utilizing a quarterback sneak on first down to, hopefully, get the football out past the one-yard line, using an off-tackle power play on second down to his team's right where his best run-blocking tackle is aligned, and then selecting a third-down play from a short list of plays he has already determined and practiced as part of his team's coming- out offensive plan. Grab-bagging a response is not a viable option in such a dire critical offensive situation. Such a scenario illustrates why a team should have a carefully planned game plan and practice plan in the first place.

The primary reason for developing a highly structured schedule is to help keep a coach on task. On the other hand, even within such careful, well-ordered planning, a coach must be sure to maintain a good degree of flexibility. Despite having a limited timeframe, he must try to address all of the various phases of an offensive game effort that can, and, often will, occur during the course of a game. The coach may discover, for example, that an hour and a half for base dropback pass protection planning might not be enough. He might find himself running over into the next planning time segment. The key point to keep in mind is that more often than not, he will often find himself not precisely on the planned schedule. Instead, he will probably notice that he is running over a specific time-planning segment or even finishing early. Truth be known, having extra time on his hands is usually never a problem, while running over a time-planning segment can be.

In reality, the main reason for running over into another time-planning segment is usually the result of the coach not keeping his eye on the clock. Another cause might be the coach not sticking to the basics for a particular game-plan segment. For example, an offensive staff might waste time trying to design new play thoughts for a third-and-seven to nine (deep medium) critical offense situation. Too often, they overlook the fact that if the new idea, or ideas, were so good, they probably would have incorporated those (pass) plays in their base offense to begin with.

Before spending time trying to design new plays to counter a particular situation, the coach should first check what has already been good to him in his own ready-list arsenal in that specific situation. Then he should review what pass plays have been good to him against the coverages his upcoming opponent's defense has shown to employ in that situation in the scouting report. The coach should start from within his own existing offense, rather than contemplating some possible new possibilities that have originated in someone else's offense that he has seen on video.

For example, his team might have run the Y-option pass play nine times this season in the third-and-seven to nine situation and has been successful on eight of them. Should he fear that his opponent will probably be looking for a Y-option pass in this situation and be ready to jump it? Perhaps. Then again, if he has been effective eight of nine times this year using the Y-option, what makes him think that his next opponent can suddenly be able to stop it? Perhaps, all he needs to do is employ that same Y-option pass play and disguise its usage with a different formation or with a shift and/or motion.

A coach should always remember that while what he does is important, how he does what he does is far more important. All factors considered, the more a coach can stick to his own basics—what he, his staff, and his players know and can perform best—the more success he will probably have.

Keeping an eye on the clock and sticking to what the offensive coordinator does best with regard to his basics can definitely help him to stay on track in his effort to adhere to his weekly day-by-day game and practice plan schedule. On the other hand, if he does run over in a planning segment, he shouldn't panic. He should simply realize that he now has fewer minutes from his usable bank of hours and minutes to put together his all-important game plan and practice plans. In reality, the harder he works to stay on schedule, the better he will become at it. Eventually, he will develop his own inner clock telling him that it's time to get moving—it's time to move on. At some point in time, he will learn to say "O.K., we've watched enough video. What plays do we want to use in this situation?"

Using Staff Experts

One viable way to enhance a coach's efforts to focus on sound time management when he's attempting to put together an effective game plan and efficient practice plans is to utilize staff experts. Figure 1-2, for example, shows that Monday morning has a four and a half hour block of time allotted to run and run-option game planning, including an hour-long segment devoted to base and play-action passing. All factors considered, a head coach or offensive coordinator may want to include all of the offensive staff in such meetings. This step will enable the head coach or his offensive coordinator to "ride herd" on the offensive assistants in an effort to monitor and maintain tight control of the offensive staff's efforts. This approach can be particularly appropriate if the staff contains a significant number of young, inexperienced coaches. When working all together, as a single offensive staff group, to address a specific portion of the offensive game plan, this procedure gives the offensive coordinator the ability to instruct his staff as well as the capacity to prepare a well-crafted strategy for identifying the best possible way to handle a particular play calling situation. This method also enables the offensive coordinator to be confident that all plans have been put together to his personal satisfaction, rather than leaving important parts of the game plan in the hands of coaches who may not be quite ready to handle such responsibility. It is also important to keep in mind that this particular way of creating game and practice plans may not be the best process for a coach to utilize the limited amount of hours and minutes he has available to complete the task.

Another possible method for developing game and practice plans that can be employed is to generate "staff experts." Far too often, staff coaches actually watch all of the relevant videos together, as well as do all of their planning together. On the other hand, when a limited amount of time for planning exists, this approach can be counterproductive. The key issue is whether a team's offensive line coach and, perhaps, its backfield coach really need to be in on the overall video study and really need to help devise the strategy for the play-action pass part of the game plan or the offensive's dropback pass and quick-pass game phase of the game plan. Obviously, while the offensive line coach, or whatever assistant might be involved, might learn a lot about the team's pass-pattern action, it could easily be argued that this is not the time of the year that a coach wants his offensive line coach to learn such a lesson. In reality, the truly important singular focus of the staff must be to develop an effective game plan, within the confines of the severely limited amount of time that the staff has available during an in-seasonal game week.

In fact, developing and using "staff experts" can enhance a coach's efforts to maximize his time management usage. The schedule detailed in Figure 1-2 illustrates how this strategy might be wisely employed. For example, during the four and a half hours allotted on Monday morning, the offensive line and backfield coaches could go off together to study the game video of the upcoming opponent and put together a *suggested* base run, run option, and pass protection plan. Simultaneously, the quarterback and wide receiver coaches could assemble somewhere to work on putting together a *suggested* pass pattern attack, including anti-blitz passing. Concurrently, the tight end coach could work on possible goal line and formationing responses and actions.

As a coordinator, I want to be the one individual who studies the opponent's previous game videos from a generalist's point of view. I want to scrutinize and evaluate the actual flow of other offenses as they attempt to attack our next opponent's defensive structure. For example, I like to study and want to determine how our next opponent tries to defense balanced two-by-two offensive structures or an unbalanced three-by-one structure, as illustrated in Figures 1-3 and 1-4.

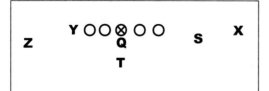

Figure 1-3. How does an opponent defense a two-by-two offensive structure?

Figure 1-4. How does an opponent defense a three-by-one offensive structure?

More importantly, I want to ascertain how the defense of our next opponent might try to defend the structure of the offensive formations that my team is going to use. Hopefully, such knowledge would include how the defense might react to shifting and motioning action that might otherwise change the structure of our offensive formation, given that we incorporate such shifting and motioning concepts into our offense.

One way or the other, over the course of a season, or seasons, individual coaches can develop expertise in specific parts of the offense's game plan. For example, a certain coach might be the team's blitz pick-up expert. Another coach might be the goal line/short yardage expert or the red zone/black zone or third-and-long expert.

It is important to keep in mind that these assistant coaches don't necessarily have to dictate what a coordinator might plan to do in certain game situations. Those coaches, however, will be the individuals who have the responsibility of studying how the weekly opponent's defense will try to stop a particular phase of the offense, for example, the base-run game. These coaches should be expected to propose run plays from the team's overall run-play ready list arsenal that they feel will best achieve success, utilizing the formations, shifts, and motions that they feel can best facilitate those specific base runs. In a similar vein, these "experts" can also suggest which plays to avoid and why. Subsequently, in a scheduled time period, after finalizing the base-run plan, they will present their video study findings to the entire offensive staff. Then, the staff can make any suggestions for additions, deletions, adjustments, or changes needed to their recommended plan. It then becomes the offensive coordinator's job to put his final stamp of approval on the final plan, dictating any last minute additions, deletions, adjustments, or changes that he may deem necessary.

Using offensive staff experts allows for a much more defined assignment of game and practice plan responsibilities. Each coach is given his part of the offensive game plan for which he is responsible. Some coaches may initially need help to learn how to properly analyze an opponent's defensive blitz package or two-minute defense. As a season gets rolling, however, it can be amazing to see how much individual coaches can develop their skills in this critical aspect of coaching.

Using (and developing) an offensive staff expert's concept can be an excellent time management tool. It should always be remembered, however, that the offensive coordinator is the person who has the final say in deciding how to make all parts of the offenses' game plan fit. This responsibility is why this particular coach has the title of "coordinator." It is also very important to keep in mind that whenever a team decides to utilize "staff experts" that the coordinator must be sure that members of his offensive coaching staff are experienced and qualified enough to take on such independent game-planning duties.

2

Day One: Game Week Game and Practice Plan Preparation

As was detailed previously in the hypothetical example, it is 11:30 a.m. on Sunday morning (or 7:30 a.m. on Saturday morning), the day after the game the previous day. Hopefully, the coach and his staff are excited about beginning a new week's work. Everyone has put that great victory (all factors considered, all victories are great) aside and is getting on with their preparation for next week's game and opponent. If his team lost yesterday, he has to find the inner strength to rally his troops (his coaching staff and his players) and prepare for the next challenge at hand.

As adverse as a defeat can be, he, as a coach, must be sure that last week's defeat has minimal effect, if any, on his new effort to prepare for the team's next opponent. This factor is true no matter how difficult the challenge of that next game might be. What might seem to be an earth-shattering, extremely negative defeat one week can be just as quickly turned into a season momentum-producing win the next. The coach must be sure that he and his staff are not responsible for holding the team back from winning its next game because of staff negativism from the previous week's loss. All factors considered, the success of a team's season will be determined by the results of 10 or 11 games—not one defeat or, even, one victory. If last week's game ended in defeat, the coach should do whatever he can to correct the mistakes made in that game and enthusiastically move on to his next opponent. If his team won, the coach should keep the ball rolling by building on that success. The primary key to winning is attitude—a positive, winning attitude.

Putting Yesterday's Game to Rest

Across the country, on almost every competitive level, the first thing a staff does on the day after a game is to review and grade the video footage from the previous day's game. As a rule, most staffs will initially break down into their individual positional groupings and grade their player's performances. The quarterback coach will grade the quarterbacks. The wide receiver coach will grade the wide receivers, and so forth. If the team has two offensive line coaches, one might grade the center and guards, while the other line coach might grade the tackles and tight ends.

With regard to grading individual performances, a variety of grading methods can be used. A number of coaches employ a +/− grading system, giving a + for positive execution and a − for negative execution. In such a system, coaches often give a double ++ grade for great performance and a double -- grade for an extremely poor play performance, such as a missed assignment, as illustrated in Figure 2-1.

1. +	8. +	15. +	22. +
2. +	9. -	16. +	23. +
3. -	10. +	17. +	24. +
4. +	11. +	18. -	25. +
5. +	12. +	19. +	
6. ++	13. +	20. +	
7. +	14. +	21. +	

Figure 2-1. Plus/minus individual game grading system

To determine a player's percentage grade, the coach simply divides the total number of pluses by the total combined number of pluses and minuses. Using Figure 2-1 as an example, in 25 plays the player earned 23 pluses (remember that he earned two pluses on the sixth play) and three minuses, for a total combined number of 26 pluses and minuses. Figure 2-2 demonstrates the percentage grade calculation.

$$\frac{23+}{\div\ 26\ \text{total}\ (23+\ +\ 3-)}$$
$$88\%$$

Figure 2-2. Determining a player's individual game grade

Some coaches give two grades—one grade for execution/performance and a second grade for effort. The underlying premise of this approach is that great effort is needed to have an exceptional performance and that poor effort will, almost always, result in a lackluster performance.

Once the video is graded and the individual grades have been determined, the entire staff (offensive, defensive, and special teams) will normally review their unit and positional grades. As a rule, each of the coordinators will provide an overview of each unit's performance to the head coach. In addition, individual game awards are usually determined in this meeting.

For the rest of the afternoon, the offensive and defensive staffs will meet separately, as a group, to view the previous day's game video as a unit. As a rule, each positional coach will verbally note any particularly good or poor performance of one of their players. Having each offensive unit view the video provides the coordinator and possibly the head coach with an opportunity to make their comments.

The head coach may prefer to hold the full staff game-and-positional-grade review meeting *after* he views the game video of each unit (offense, defense, and special teams) of the game on the previous day with the staff of each unit. The basic premise of this approach is that conducting a full staff meeting at a later time to discuss overall unit and individual position evaluations will be more accurate, after the offensive, defensive, and kicking game staffs have already watched the video.

View the Previous Day's Video of the Next Opponent

After the staff has had a dinner break, a desired step is to have the offensive coaches watch the game video together, as an offensive staff, from the previous day of the defense of the upcoming week's opponent. This situation is the one pragmatic opportunity to view video of the next opponent together, as a staff. Such a viewing can be of great value.

Such a session could start by having the team's graduate assistant and/or scout squad coaches give a brief overview of the upcoming opponent's defense, information compiled while they were breaking down video of the opponent from the previous week's game. For example, such a quick overview of the next opponent's defense by the graduate assistant coach (or coaches assigned to break down an opponent's game video from the week before) might go something like the following:

> *"The Tigers play a 4-3 over or under front defense. Their over and under front usage doesn't seem to have a particular pattern. They just seem to mix the two front structures continually during the course of a game. Movement of their front four defensive linemen is a constant. They like to slant and angle their defensive line, tied in with outside-*

linebacker pressures. Two- and three-man twist stunts are also a major part of their defensive package.

Their base coverage is quarters coverage, which they use extensively. They provide coverage variety by occasionally using cover 2 or quarter-quarter-half coverage. They like to use Tampa-2 coverage on passing-down situations.

Their defensive coordinator likes to pressure (blitz)—almost always with just his linebackers. He rarely blitzes with his secondary defenders. Most of his linebacker pressures come off the edge (to the outside). When they pressure, they almost always use cover 0 (four-across man coverage) or man-free coverage."

Such a quick, five-to-ten minute, relatively brief introduction of what coaches should expect to see on the video that the staff is scheduled to view helps to quickly get their minds focused on the defense that they will be facing from their next opponent, based on video footage of the defense utilized by their upcoming opponent in its previous games.

Having the offensive staff view the previous day's game video together can have a multitude of values. In conjunction with the graduate assistant's or scout squad coach's introductory presentation, this approach can provide the offensive coordinator with the ability to be sure that everyone on the offensive staff is "on the same page" when it comes to analyzing the upcoming opponent's defense. If the staff was to immediately break down individually or into small groups, a difference of opinion might exist with regard to the type of structure of the defense and/or in the way that the defensive front, stunts, blitzes, and coverages are called. If that difference of opinion were to occur, the coaches could go off in different directions concerning what they believe that the next opponent's defense will be doing.

In addition, this procedure enables the offensive staff to check and understand the terminology used by the graduate assistant or scout squad coaches, as they were breaking down the game video of the next opponent's defense. Giving a stunt or blitz a new name is fine, just as long as every coach on the staff knows exactly what that term or name denotes. Proper and consistent communication is paramount to a well-coordinated game plan effort.

Having the coaches view the game video of the next opponent's previous game can also provide the staff and the coordinator with an opportunity to correct any possible mistakes that might have been made by the graduate assistant coaches or scout squad coaches as they broke down that video footage. As stated previously, it is extremely important that everyone on the staff goes into its planning week efforts "on the same page." Planning mistakes must be avoided. One of the best ways to do that is to make sure everyone on the staff has a consistent understanding of the defensive structure that the offense will be trying to attack.

In addition, watching the previous day's video of the next opponent's defense can give the staff a viable opportunity to develop a better understanding of the skill-set of the personnel that they will be facing in their next game. Such an analysis can provide invaluable information. For example, planning special adjustments to stop an opponent's super star defensive end would be fruitless if that defensive end had recently sprained an ankle and would definitely be out for the upcoming game. In reality, the coach might quickly determine that instead of running away from that super star weakside end, he might want to focus his run efforts directly at the super star's replacement, who is perceived as being a significantly weaker performer. As such, viewing the previous day's game video of the upcoming opponent can provide a coach and his staff with the most up-to-date information concerning what personnel the opponent's defense will be employing against him.

In the final phase of the meeting in which the full staff collectively views game footage of the defense of next week's opponent, the graduate assistant coaches and/or scout squad coaches could provide an evaluation and an analysis of what they feel are the strengths and the weaknesses of the defense of the upcoming opponent. This report is undertaken from both a structural and personnel basis. For example, their summation might go as follows: "They are going to load the box by bringing down their quarters- coverage safeties, when we're in two-back or "H" back personnel, in an attempt to shut down the run game. The safeties are going to align low in an effort to produce an unblocked defender." This feedback is the type of information that a coach is looking for in such a briefing meeting. They might also add that: "Number 21, their corner who always plays into the boundary, is a super player. He's a *great* cover corner. We should stay away from him. Their field corner, number 5, is pretty decent, but is short. He has trouble when isolated on tall receivers, especially when they go deep."

From a structural standpoint, a coach would want to know something like the following "Their quarters coverage matches up well with our two-by two (offensive) formations, but is consistently a defender short to the strongside when facing three-by-one (offensive) formations." From a weakness and strength evaluation, a coach should try to take advantage of a defense's weaknesses and to identify ways to attack a defense's strengths.

All factors considered, attacking an opponent's weaknesses is easiest. On the other hand, finding ways to attack a defense's strengths is typically much more difficult to do. Carefully studying video and having a creative mindset can help to, literally, put an offense in a position to frustrate and disturb a defense's playing tempo by finding ways to attack its strengths. For example, an All-American-quality linebacker may be great, because he runs and pursues to the football extremely well when an opponent's run or passes are to his outside or backside. That same "big time" linebacker, however, may be quite average when the football is run directly at him.

The aforementioned illustrate the type of evaluations and analyses a coach is looking for and needs. Such a short, to-the-point, evaluation and analyses briefing meeting can help get the entire offensive staff to immediately focus on the next opponent's defense. Not only can such a focus help the offensive staff to expeditiously disregard the previous week's game plan, it can also facilitate getting the staff to quickly go on the attack with regard to game planning for their next opponent.

3

Creating a Base, Par Down Situation Game Plan

The Big Three of Offensive Game Planning

It's about 6:45 a.m. on Monday morning. The coach is only a few more minutes drive from work, and his mind is already starting to focus on his first task at hand: the start of his game-planning efforts for the defense of this week's opponent. His offensive game-planning efforts are organizationally divided into three major game-planning segments: his base, par down offense; his third-down offense; and his red zone offense, which includes deep red zone offense (beyond the +20), basic red zone offense (+20 yard line and in), black zone offense (inside the +10 yard line where the offense can no longer get a first down), goal line offense, and two-point play offense.

While a few additional game-planning elements should also be addressed, such as second-and-long offense, coming-out offense, four-minute slow-slow offense, and two-minute hurry-hurry offense, focusing on the so-called "big three" of game planning (base, par down offense; third-down offense, and red zone offense) covers the three most important aspects of game planning offensive play. Experience indicates these "big three" game-planning facets will, game in and game out, have the most effect on the ability of an offense to perform well, thereby helping the team in its effort to be victorious. That factor doesn't mean that game planning and practicing the two-minute, hurry-hurry offense, for example, isn't extremely important. On the other hand, a team will consistently employ its base, par down offense and its third-down offense game in and game out. Just as likely, it will also consistently be in need of its all-important and quite essential red zone offense.

When offenses fail, critics will often point to lack of effectiveness on third-down situations, particularly those in the red zone. In reality, a lack of effectiveness on base, par down offense, as well as in such offensive aspects as four-minute slow-slow (sometimes referred to on occasion as use-up-the-clock) offense, can also have a critical impact on the team's ability to be productive offensively. It should be noted, however, that when a team is addressing such an important game-planning need, such as its four-minute, slow-slow offense, it often finds itself combing through the list of run plays in its base, par down offense in an attempt to identify run plays that will help prevent its ball-carrying running backs from running out of bounds so that they don't stop the clock, when the situation desperately demands that they keep the clock running.

Base, Par Down Offense

As has previously been discussed, the coach's initial starting point for creating the new week's offensive game plan is his base, par down game plan. The term "base" refers to the desire of the coach to use what he feels are the basic plays in his offense (i.e., "hangs its hat on"). As a rule, base offense includes a team's base runs, play-action passes, and all of its base quick and dropback passes. (In general, the quick-pass game is the three-step drop pass game, while the dropback pass game refers to the five- and seven-step drop pass game.) The term "par down offense" encompasses first-and-ten or second-and-medium (i.e., three to six yards) to second-and-short (one to two yards) down situations. For the most part, defenses tend to treat first-and-ten and second-and-medium to short-yardage situations similarly, with regard to how they attempt to defense them. Accordingly, they can be lumped into one collective category, called par downs, and one large play call plan can be devised to address par down offensive situations.

It is important to keep in mind that the phrase "for the most part" does not mean "always." While teams treat first-and-ten to second and medium-to-short yardage situations similarly, most coaches use computer breakdown scouting to analyze the individual breakdowns of first-and-ten, second-and-medium (three to six yards) and second-and-short (one to two yards) situations separately, one after the other. Teams also analyze first-and-five situations in this scouting effort, if any occurred. Coaches want to be certain that their generalization of the grouping of all of these situations into one "par" down situational call grouping is correct. If either the second-and-medium (three to six yards) or the second-and-short (one to two yards) yardage situations are significantly different with regard to the type of defensive play call that is employed, then a separate play call category is created for those particular second-down play call situations.

Creating a Base, Par Down Offense Game Plan

A coach should start out his new week's opponent game preparation by creating his base, par down offense game plan. This step is undertaken because it is one of the most critically important facets of his team's overall weekly offensive plan to engage the defense of this week's opponent. Base, par down offense game planning includes the runs, the base pass protections, the play-action passes, and all other passes that will be employed on par downs.

A number of coaches believe that this aspect is the simplest part of the game plan to devise. Simply stated, those coaches would claim, "Just use your best, most effective runs and passes on par downs." When a coach does that, he starts out with a simple, basic part of his game plan, one that is relatively easy to create and that should not normally have to take a lot of his time. Frankly speaking, that's not a bad idea.

It is recommended, however, that a coach should take such par down game planning a definite step further. A major goal for most coaches, year in and year out, is to have a dominant, high-scoring offense. To do that, the offense must be on the field for as many snaps as possible during the course of the game, which will give the team the best chance to be successful, week in and week out. To accomplish such a goal, the coach must have a *great* plan for his team's par down attack, not just a good one.

A major offensive goal for many collegiate teams every year is to be in the top ten in the country for the least number of "three-and-outs." Three-and-out action is one of the most devastating factors to offensive production that exists. To avoid this action from occurring, players and coaches have to be taught that three-and-outs are *not acceptable* and should be avoided at all costs. If the coach wants offensive momentum that produces lots of plays and lots of scoring opportunities, he should utilize plays and formations, shifts, and motions that will help him to be as successful as possible on par downs. Such action can greatly help promote consistent offensive momentum. Truth be known, it's hard to generate offensive momentum if his team is going three-and-out a majority of the time.

In reality, most coaches do, in fact, focus on using their best, most efficient runs, pass protections, play-action passes, and other pass-actions on par downs. Coaches can go a definite step further, however, by developing a plan that employs those plays from personnel plans and formations (with possible shifts and motions) that help give such plays their best chance of being successful. If a play gains five yards on first down, the team will be in great shape, with two downs left to gain another first down. On second-and-five, a short two-yard gain will still help put the offense in a reasonably manageable third-and short/medium situation.

Coaches should make every effort to determine what specific personnel plans, formations, shifts, and motions can help to facilitate the best possible attack against the defenses they expect to see from their upcoming, next opponent. One viable way to ascertain this information is to use the best plays of the offense to hypothetically fix upon a possible solution. Coaches, for example, should look to see how usage of their personnel plans, multiple formations, shifts, and motions might create personnel weakness isolations of the defense or make defensive structural weaknesses known, as the defense tries to defense such variations of the offensive structure.

Most coaches believe in having their offense cause a multiplicity of problems for a defense. As such, they try to find the best ways to execute a limited number of run and pass plays. In reality, extensive and varied multiple use of personnel plans, formations, shifts, and motion from play-to-play and series-to-series can make it extremely difficult for defenses to get a fix on what offenses are trying to do as they attempt to attack a defense. The philosophy is that many coaches want to make defenses and, more importantly, defensive players to think. They don't want to observe linebackers in their stances, up on their toes, ready to strike like a coiled up rattlesnake. Instead, they prefer to see linebackers yelling to their front to make proper adjustments to a shift or a motion, frantically directing their teammates to align properly. The same set of circumstances can be said for the secondary. When coaches see secondary defenders acting confused in response to a different personnel plan, a strange formation, or a shift and/or motion, they then know that their offense is in better control of the situation.

As a rejoinder to the aforementioned, some coaches might declare, "But coach, we have an opposite philosophy. We only use one formation, aligned to the right or left, so that we can see exactly what the defense is going to try to do and then call the play from the sideline to the players on the field. Is that wrong?" Of course, that's not wrong. Those coaches are articulating one of the newest trends in college and high school football as a part of spread offensive thinking. In reality, one of the primary purposes of this book is to help a coach, regardless of what offensive system his team employs—the wing-T, the wishbone, the I, or the spread, to effectively game and practice plan.

Varied Personnel Plan Usage

The use of varied and multiple personnel plans has increasingly become an integral part of the concepts underlying a multiple offense attack approach. This factor has had a major impact on the efforts of coaches to do whatever they can to ensure that the plays on their game-plan, play call list will actually be successful. In response, many coaches use large sideline cards to announce to the defense what offensive personnel structure is coming on to the field for the next scrimmage down. For example, "12" signals for one back, two tight end, two wide receiver personnel plan, while "11" signals for one back, one tight end, and three wide receivers. A careful analysis of how defenses react to the variety of ways offenses employ their personnel often shows that the defense may only use one or two particular defensive fronts and/or coverages for each of those personnel plan groupings.

Nor surprisingly, all coaches would love to know exactly what a defense is going to do in a particular situation, or at least have a good idea of what they are going to do, when they're making a play call. These responses are the type of defensive keys that coaches look for when they analyze a defense's base, par down defense video breakdowns or, for that matter, any other play call game-plan consideration. Figure 3-1 provides a listing of how offense and defenses have come to designate (number) offensive personnel plans.

- "0" personnel—(no) backs, (no) tight ends, (5) wide receivers
- "10" personnel—(1) back, (no) tight ends, (4) wide receivers
- "11" personnel—(1) back, (1) tight end, (3) wide receivers
- "12" personnel— (1) back, (2) tight ends, (2) wide receivers
- "13" personnel—(1) back, (3) tight ends, (1) wide receiver
- "14" personnel—(1) back, (4) tight ends, (no) wide receivers
- "20" personnel—(2) backs, (no) tight ends, (3) wide receivers
- "21" personnel—(2) backs, (1) tight end, (2) wide receivers
- "22" personnel—(2) backs, (2) tight ends, (1) wide receiver

Figure 3-1. Numerical personnel plan designations

Analyzing an Opponent's Defense

At this point, the staff begins to devise the team's base, par down offensive run play call plan by analyzing formational breakdown videos of the defense of this week's opponent in par down situations. For the most part, they analyze videos of recent games that the upcoming opponent has just played. They also evaluate games of the next opponent's defense against teams whose offenses are similar to theirs. Obviously, they don't want to spend time analyzing and creating a base, par down offense play call game plan, based on information from a game in which the opposition's defense is defending a triple option offense, if their team runs a pro style, run-and-pass attack. A defense would, most likely, defend a triple-option, run-oriented offense very differently than it would a pro-style offense. As a result, paying attention to such an opponent's defensive efforts against the triple option might actually be counterproductive. Such study could give incorrect data concerning what type of defensive designs to expect come game time.

Coaches should analyze, from their video breakdowns, all of the defensive fronts, coverages, line games, stunts, and blitzes employed by the opponent against formations that are identical, or somewhat similar, to the ones that their team uses. For example, they would analyze every defensive effort against a three-wide receiver, doubles formation that is similar to their own three-receiver, doubles formation sets. More often than not, they will be able to analyze 15 to 20 sets that are almost identical to the ones their team uses. On the other hand, they might find a similar number of formations that are structurally similar to the ones their team uses, as illustrated in Figures 3-2 and 3-3.

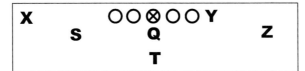

Figure 3-2. A three-wide receiver, doubles formation

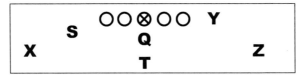

Figure 3-3. A similar three-wide receiver, doubles formation

It is important to note that an analysis of the defensive responses against the three-wide receiver, doubles formation shown in Figure 3-2 can provide coaches with pertinent information, even through the actual offensive formations used may be slightly different from the one they might employ, as detailed in Figure 3-3.

Sometimes, coaches may only find two or three examples of their opponent's defensing offensive formations that are the same, or similar, to the formations that their teams use. Although two or three similar formations, for example, may not be very much, two or three are better than none at all.

This factor can be especially relevant if coaches employ formations that they can't find other teams using against their upcoming opponent. What do they do then? All factors considered, they should apply their upcoming opponent's defensive alignments rules that they have previously demonstrated, in general, and proceed with their base, par down offense play call game plan from that point. In other words, sometimes, coaches have to make their best educated guess from the information that they have available.

In the attack-plan analysis of each formation structure their teams use, coaches should attempt to determine which plays, from their offense, will have the greatest chance of being successful. As such, they can devise their base, par down offense play call game plan by trying to analyze the weaknesses of the defense and utilize plays from their base, par down offense arsenal that they believe can best attack such weaknesses. On the other hand, they can also employ plays from their base, par down offense arsenal that they feel effectively attacks what is considered to be the strength of a defense. For example, a sell-out, double-team block on a star defensive end or a trap block on a talented, penetrating defensive tackle can often be effective in attacking a defense's strength. Furthermore, such a strategy may also help to break down a defense's confidence. In reality, an offense may try to do both.

The bottom line is that a defense, on par-down situations, will attempt to defense the formations and plays that an offenses uses in a certain way. By analyzing and studying the way an opponent's defense responds (i.e., attacks) the same or similar formations and plays that their teams utilize can provide very useful information. As a consequence, coaches can put together a base, par down offense play call game plan that can effectively attack their opponent's defensive efforts on par down and second-and-long situations.

Start With a Base, Par Down Run-Game Plan

As a rule, most coaches start their base, par down offense play call planning with their run game. Their run game staff specialists (the offensive line coach, the running backs coach, and, perhaps, the tight end coach) work to find three to five different ways to run their inside-zone run play and two, perhaps three, different ways to run their outside-zone run play, if these are often the two top run plays in their base run-game arsenal. The term "different ways" of running inside- and outside-zone run plays refers to the varied use of different formations, shifts, and motions. In addition, this approach can be extremely effective when quarterbacks employ check techniques on the line of scrimmage to help get the offense into a sound play, be it a run or a pass.

Once coaches determine what their best formational and line of scrimmage quarterback-check applications are of the base run plays that can most effectively be employed against their next opponent, they can then develop a balanced, effective run-game plan. For example, while counter run plays may not have looked great against the defense of their team's next opponent, they may still feel that they must utilize some form of counter-action to take advantage of their opponent's tendency to overpursue to the flow of the football.

In that instance, coaches should definitely be sure to *carefully* plan to utilize counter run-play action as a part of their base run-play arsenal. As such, they should work hard to find at least one counter-action run play that would provide them with a formational advantage that presents the defense of their upcoming opponent with counter-action problems.

Personally, I would probably not run all three of the counter-run action plays that we have in our base-run play arsenal. Instead, I would probably pick the one, maybe two, counter-run plays from our base-run play arsenal that I feel has the best chance of succeeding against that particular defense.

The bottom line is that coaches must ensure that whatever counter-run play they decide to run is given the proper amount of practice and coaching time needed to best help it be successful come game time. It is also important to remember that counter-action does not just have to mean an inside counter-run play. It could be an outside counter trap or a counter sweep play. It could also entail a reverse run, a bootleg, or a naked bootleg run/pass play.

A coach may have an excellent trap run play-action in his playbook. On the other hand, the defense that the coach is going up against this week is not the penetrating, upfield rush defense that he would like to see to help make his trap game successful. If that were the case, that coach would probably put his trap play or trap series on the shelf for that week. The key is for the coach to use the plays in his base run-play arsenal that he feels will best help him successfully attack his opponent's defense and enable him to have his best chance of succeeding in critical par down situations.

One issue that often arises is whether a coach should employ option action, sprint-outs, and trick plays on par downs. Why not? … especially if those plays are a part of his base offensive package. On the other hand, however, he should try hard to not stray too far from the underlying premise of his base offensive package. While adding a new run or pass play might well be a viable answer to a pressing game-plan need, the coach needs to ask himself if that particular play is so good, why was it not incorporated as an intrinsic part of his offense long ago, when he was initially putting his playbook together.

Three practice days for a new play is not a particularly significant amount of time to teach, coach, and practice a new play. A coach should remember that the bottom line is not, necessarily, what he does, but *how* he does what he does. Personally, I'd rather run my best run or pass play from a different formation with, perhaps, a disguise via a shift or motion than to rely on a brand new play in a critical-down situation. As play callers everywhere can attest, *every* down is a critical down *not* to be wasted.

Create a Tight, Condensed Base, Par Down Run-Game Plan

Although coaches might expend a very intent and focused amount of time in developing their initial base, par down offense game plan, they should be careful to make sure that their plan is tight and condensed. They should try to establish their *best*, but definitely limited, base run, pass, and subsequent pass-protection plan for their base, par down offense play call list and then get on with it. They're much better having a smaller base, par down offense plan that best provides them with the ability to expend the appropriate amount of practice time that is needed to get their base, par down offense *run-* and *pass*-game plans ready to succeed.

It often appears that too many offensive coordinators and offensive staffs put far too much time and effort into their base offensive thinking. As a result, they often end up with *too much* base offense, which requires an exorbitant amount of preparation time during the course of the week's game planning, practice planning, and actual practice time. In the time-related limitations of base, par down offense planning and preparation, coaches should be asking themselves, "… what, in our total offensive ready list arsenal, do we feel will best attack both the strengths and the weaknesses of the opponent's defense that we will be facing that particular game week?" As noted previously, it is essential that coaches keep their base, par down offense plan as tight and, yet, as complete as possible. They must always keep in mind to ask themselves, "What is our best stuff for par down situations? What, in our base run game (which is where we should start our base, par down offense planning), do we feel will best likely succeed against the defense that we will be facing come game time?"

Create a Tight, Condensed Base, Par Down Pass-Game Plan

After coaches have established their initial base, par down offense formational run-game plan, they next move to identifying their base, par down offense play-action pass play call plan. Then they move on to setting their quick-and-dropback pass-game play call plan for par down situations. To the degree possible, they tie their play-action pass plays to the base run-play formational combinations they have game-planned.

In general, play-action passing works best off of the run plays that the coach is going to use during the course of a game and from the formations that he has planned to use for those runs. Once a defense feels it is getting comfortable with regard to recognizing a particular formational structure (i.e., a certain run play), it may start to cheat up in its alignment to jump on such a run. This situation is the perfect time for a play-action pass off of a run play that the defense thinks is coming.

In reality, while it may be too difficult or simply not possible to have a play-action pass come off of every run play/formation combination, the greater the possible number of usages of a particular run play out of a specific formational structure, the more likely that a complementary play-action pass will be effective. Of course, the level of execution of that particular play-action pass play will also be a key factor in its success. Furthermore, executing play-action passes off of a team's most commonly used runs and the formations from which the runs are executed can provide that team with a significant advantage in helping make the play-action pass-game of that team work.

The aforementioned does not mean that a team shouldn't use a play-action pass off of runs and formations that are not a big part of its base, par down offense package. No, it doesn't! Personally, I can think of many times, throughout my career, when a particular play-action pass worked extremely well, regardless of whether we employed the run or the formation off of which we are faking. Sometimes, a play, be it a run, play-action pass or dropback pass, can be extremely effective despite the fact that it is not tied in with the rest of the game plan for that particular opponent. Why? No definitive answer exists. The answer may be as simple as because *it does*. It may be just a play that effectively works by itself, no matter what else the team does in its offensive attack.

Coaches should also determine whether their quick-pass and dropback pass games will be appropriate for their base, par down offense usage. As with their play-action game, they should look for the best quick-pass and dropback pass par down usage, in combination with the best sets, formations shifts, and motions that they employ. As a result, they may not always just try to throw a dropback pass on third-down situations. They might, just as easily, utilize their dropback pass game on first down, which will force the defense to have to defend as many possible offensive facets as possible on par downs.

Similar to their efforts to devise their base, par down offense run-game plan, coaches should see how their opponent's defensive formations will try to match up with the offensive formations similar to the ones that their teams use. This effort should address several basic questions. For example, what coverages do their opponents use on par down situations? What defensive fronts do they employ? Do they blitz on par downs? How often do they blitz on par downs? What type of blitzes do they use? Do they zone blitz? … man blitz? What formation (with possible shifts and motions) would best give the defenses that the opponents employ on par downs problems?

Another key factor that should be determined is what type of pass plays have hurt the opponent's defense. Similar to their efforts to generate their base, par run-game plan, coaches should look to see how their usage of multiple formations, shifts, and motions might create personnel weakness isolations or defensive structural weaknesses in the defense as it responds to the array of possible offensive variations.

At this point, coaches should not get overly involved in incorporating their quick-pass and dropback pass games into their base, par down offense game plan. Initially, they should try to identify pass-game plays that, all factors considered, jump out at them with regard to their possible successful usage as a part of their base, par down offense game plan. In general, their initial base, par down offense pass plan is usually purposely very small. Their decision-making process concerning what pass-game plays to include is relatively straightforward. What are the very best quick pass game plays that they want to use? What are the very best dropback passes? … roll-out passes? … sprint-out passes?

Most coaches generally prefer to have a condensed list of base, par down offense passes because they want to emphasize the base runs and play-action passes that they have determined will best attack their opponent's defense on par downs. As a rule, adding a lot of quick passes to the list of base, par down offense play calls in their game plan could clutter up and, perhaps, be counterproductive to their offensive efforts. On the other hand, some coaches *love* to quick-pass on par downs. In fact, that's a big part of their play call thinking. As a consequence, they keep their base, par down offense play call list to a manageable number by limiting the number of dropback passes on it. They accomplish that goal by initially determining what three, or four, *very best* dropback passes should be put on their base, par down offense pass play call list and then stop at that point.

Before finalizing their base, par down offense pass-game plan, most coaches prefer that the next major segment of our total offensive game plan—third-down—is completed first. When they finish their third-down offense game plan, they then try to determine what part of their third-down offense pass-game plan could also be effectively employed in their base, par down offense game plan. As a result, they would be employing many of the same key play calls for their third-down offense game plan for both situations. In turn, because this situation would help reduce the overall number of quick- and dropback pass-game plays that they would employ, they would have a relatively tight, total game-plan, play call list of plays that would need to be coached and practiced.

One very important philosophical concept should, again, guide coaches in their efforts to devise a total offensive game plan for an opponent—while *what* they do *is* important, *how* they do what they do is *far more* important. The *more* coaches incorporate in their total game plan for an opponent, the *more diluted* that plan can become. A team only has so much practice time. The more plays it has in its arsenal, the less time it will have to prepare and practice each of those plays. As noted previously, coaches should strive for developing a tight, condensed total game plan that allows the plan to be well-taught and well-practiced.

Another key concept that coaches should keep in mind is that *if they think that they have too much quantity in any part of their offensive game plan, then they probably do*. If that is the situation, they should *reduce* the total volume of their game plan. If they feel that they might have too much in their offensive game plan, they should weed out any particularly difficult to execute plays that are in the plan or any plays that simply appear to be problematic for any reason. Doing that will almost always add a degree of freshness to their overall game plan, a situation somewhat similar to going on a quick diet and losing some unwanted weight.

Creating the Base, Par Down Offense Play Call Plan

Figure 3-4 illustrates a base, par down offense game-plan, play call list as it would appear on an offensive coordinator's play call chart. It should be noted that each call is separately listed for either left-hash or right-hash usage. If a play call is only targeted for use in the middle of the field, it is aligned on the play call chart in the middle of the base, par down offense play call plan sections. If, for any specific reason, coaches might want to execute a specific run or pass play from only the right hash, they would then list that play on the right side of the play call chart, within the appropriate grouping of base, par down offense play calls. For example, the "Bear right, 5 naked right" call is shown as a middle-of-the-field call on the sample chart.

BASE, PAR DOWN OFFENSE

RUNS

STRONG LT TWINS 47	STRONG RT TWINS 46
STRONG PRO RT SWEEP RT	STRONG PRO LT SWEEP LT
ZOOM WEAK LT TWINS 37 COUNTER	ZOOM WEAK RT TWINS 36 COUNTER
WING LT TWINS 21 TRAP	WING RT TWINS 20 TRAP
GUN SPREAD RT READ OPTION RT	GUN SPREAD LT READ OPTION LT
WING GUN SLOT RT 48 SHOVEL OPTION	WING GUN SLOT LT 49 SHOVEL OPTION
ACE RT 22/23 CHECK-WITH-ME	ACE LT 22/23 CHECK-WITH-ME
TRIPS LT 22 CHECK 90	TRIPS RT 23 CHECK 90
SHIFT UNBALANCED RT 46	SHIFT UNBALANCED LT 47
DOUBLES LT Z FLY 23	DOUBLES RT Z FLY 22
DOUBLE RT S FLY 20 TRAP	DOUBLES LT S FLY 21 TRAP
WEAK LT TWINS ZIP-ZAP 23 LEAD	WEAK RT TWINS ZIP-ZAP 22 LEAD
ACE RT OVER 24/25 CHECK-WITH-ME	ACE LT OVER 24/25 CHECK-WITH-ME
WING RT RETURN 24 FORCE	WING LT RETURN 25 FORCE

PASS

ZOOM STRONG TWINS LT FAKE 23 FLOOD	ZOOM STRONG TWINS RT TAKE 22 FLOOD
WG RT RETURN ATLANTA 24 Y SQUARE	WG LT RETURN ATLANTA 25 Y SQUARE

BEAR RT 5 NAKED RT

TREY RT 23 NAKED RT SOLID	TREY LT 22 NAKED LT SOLID
DOUBLES LT 93	DOUBLES RT 93
TREY RT 90 DOUBLE IN	TREY LT 90 DOUBLE IN
STRONG PRO RT 71 F ANGLE	STRONG PRO LT 71 F ANGLE
DOUBLES LT SOCKET 147 SMASH	DOUBLES RT SOCKET 247 SMASH
TREY RT 140 Y STREAK	TREY LT 240 Y STREAK

Figure 3-4. Base, par down offense game-plan, play call list

The ratio of runs to passes that teams want to adhere to during the course of the game tends to vary from team to team. Philosophically, for example, I personally prefer that the base, par down offense play call plan encompasses a 60/40 run/pass ratio. This approach reflects my philosophy. Other teams may think differently. Their run/pass ratio philosophy, for example, may be 50/50 or 40/60 run to pass. In fact, their underlying philosophy might be 10 percent run and 90 percent pass. The central goal for most coaches on base, par down offense situations is to be in manageable third-and-short (i.e., one to two yards) situations or third-and short-medium (three to six yards) situations if they have not already earned a first down on the first two plays of a new down series.

Another primary objective for most coaches is to have the fewest negative-yardage offensive plays over the course of a season. In my situation, such an achievement would lend credence to our approach of using our best par down runs, play-action passes, quick-game passes, and dropback passes for par down situations in an approximate 60/40 run-to-pass ratio. On the other hand, if I were to discover during the course of a game that our run game is getting the job done to a greater degree, I would certainly increase our run-game usage, comparatively speaking. The bottom line is that coaches should employ the base runs, play-action passes, quick-game passes, and dropback passes (or any other type of run- or pass-action) that will help their teams succeed on par downs.

Second-and-Long Offense Situation Game Plan

After their base, par down offense run-game play call plan has been determined, coaches should then focus on devising their second-and-long offense run-game plan. As discussed previously, in the section on developing the base, par down offense play call ready list, coaches should be careful to check on their base, par down offense for second-and-short-medium (i.e., three to six yards) and second-and-short (i.e., one to two yards) situations, to see if there is a great deal of difference in the defense's plan of attack (i.e., its defensive play calls) for these circumstances than how it defends when confronted by an opponent's first-and-ten par offense. If they observe much of a departure between the two defensive approaches, they should make adjustments to create separate, specific play call plans to offensively attack those two situations.

On second-and-long offense yardage situations (i.e., seven or more yards), coaches will almost always find a great variance from the type of defensive play that they will see compared to par down situations. More often than not, they will observe fronts and coverages that are focused on stopping pass-oriented play calls from the offense. For example, the defense might employ a greater amount of drop coverages with eight, or even nine, defenders dropping into coverage. The defense might also blitz more in an attempt to pressure a passing offense.

As a result, coaches might exercise second-and long offense situation play calls that are comparable to the type of play calls that they use on third-and short-medium down situations in an attempt to convert to a new first-and-ten situation. Likewise, on second-and long situations, they could call for a short pass in an attempt to create a very manageable and desirable third-and-short or short-medium-yardage-down situation.

Most coaches also like to consider using run plays that are likely to be effective in such second-and-long offense situations. For example, a trap or a draw play might be just as effective as a pass play in gaining the vital yardage needed for a new first down or to help produce a manageable third-and-short or short-medium situation. Another extremely sound alternative course of action is for coaches to simply run one of their best run plays from a formation that they feel will effectively attack the defense with any accompanying shifts and/or motions. As discussed previously, the underlying premise of such second-and-long offense situation play calling is to either gain a new first down or to put the offense in a manageable third down situation. As such, at this point it is an excellent time for a team that uses run options to utilize such option plays, whether they are double- or triple-options by design.

Similar to their earlier efforts, many coaches break their staff down to study and develop their second-and-long play call plan. Their run-game specialists (or experts) go off on their own to study how their opponent defenses second-and-long run plays and devises a second-and-long run-game play call plan to address those efforts. The same is true for the effort to create a second-and-long pass-game play call plan. The pass-game specialists also assemble separately to assess the opposition's pass-coverage designs and then to create a second-and-long offense pass-game play call plan to counter them. As always, this collective approach is undertaken to make maximum use of the time and effort of the offensive staff.

Figure 3-5 provides an example a second-and-long offense game-plan, play call list. It should be noted that this play call plan is a lot shorter than a base, par down offense situation play call plan. The reason for the relative brevity is that, hopefully, teams will typically be in base, par down offense situations (i.e., first-and-ten, second-and-short, and short-medium) a lot more than in second-and-long yardage situations.

SECOND-AND-LONG OFFENSE

RUNS

ZOOM DOUBLES LT 41 DRAW	ZOOM DOUBLES RT 40 DRAW
TRIPS LT ZIP-ZAP 21 TRAP	TRIPS RT ZIP-ZAP 20 TRAP
DIXIE LT H FLY 23	DIXIE RT H FLY 22
ACE RT OVER 22/23 CHECK-WITH-ME	ACE LT OVER 22/23 CHECK-WITH-ME

PASS

DOUBLES LT 145 S/Y CROSS	DOUBLES RT 245 S/Y CROSS
STRONG PRO RT 71 Y PIVOT	STRONG PRO LT 71 Y PIVOT
DALLAS LT 140 ACUTES	DALLAS RT 240 ACUTES
STRONG RT ZIN 71 SPACING	STRONG LT ZIN 71 SPACING
DIXIE LT H-IN SCREEN LT	DIXIE RT H-IN SCREEN RT

Figure 3-5. An example of a second-and-long offense game-plan, play call list

---

4

Creating Your Third-Down Offense Situation Game Plan

Third-Down Offense

It's still Monday, the first true planning day of the week. The previous three chapters addressed the first major segment of a total offensive game plan—the base, par down offense situation game plan and subsequently, the second-and-long offense situation game plan. The next primary segment of a total offensive game plan to be covered is the third-down offense situation game plan. From a coaching perspective, it is a reasonable goal for this particular week of their game planning week to have their base, par down offense game plan (with the subsequent second-and-long down offense game plan) and their third-down offense game plan finished by the time the staff head for home on Monday evening.

One of the primary reasons that teams typically focus their Monday game planning on base, par down offense and third-down offense is that those elements are usually two of the major underlying practice objectives they want to achieve during Tuesday's practice. As such, on Tuesdays, teams practice both their base, par down offense and their third-down offense, which enables them to install their base, par down offense— the starting point of their weekly game-planning efforts. In addition, they also install their all important third-down offense. In this instance, the reasoning is that by installing and practicing their third-down offense game plan on Tuesdays, they give themselves at least two padded practice days (usually Tuesdays and Wednesdays) for the all-important practice work on their third-down offense. Structuring their practice work in this way provides them with two days of heavy practice against their opponent's third-down defense, which frequently employs a heavy dose of blitzing.

Blitz defense, whether it's third down or any other game-down situation, can present definite problems for a pass offense, if the offense is not well-prepared to effectively block such blitzing. In addition, the pass portion of the offense must be well-prepared to execute both quick, accurate throwing and pass-catching techniques under pressure. Quite simply, an offense must have a means of dismantling a defense's efforts to blitz. If it doesn't, it could be in for a very long afternoon. On the other hand, an offense that is able to shut off a heavy defensive blitz attack, whether by blocking, quick-blitz control passing (sight adjusts, hot routes, warm routes, blitz beater routes), or a combination of both, can quickly turn such blitz action into a negative for the defense and a positive for the offense.

There's an old football coaching adage that states: "You live by the blitz, or you die by the blitz." Philosophically, almost all coaches understand that an offense must be able to handle the blitz or it will face substantial negative consequences. Not surprisingly, a key goal for an offense is to have an excellent blitz control package that can be executed to the point where the offense can burn the defense for even trying to blitz. As such, it is extremely important for teams to be able to both coach and practice their third-down offense blitz pick-up on both of their two heavy, padded practice days, Tuesdays and Wednesdays. As discussed previously, having their third-down offense game plan ready for Tuesdays gives teams the extra, vital coaching and practice day on Wednesday to target this critical factor.

Another reason why teams consider their third-down offense such an essential part of their situational game plan is that third-down offense can often be the single most important situational factor relative to their overall offensive game performance. One statistic that most teams constantly pay attention to is their third-down offense efficiency. Every time teams don't convert a third-down situation, they are going to give up the possession of the football to the opposition, unless they're in reasonable field position to attempt a field goal.

In most instances, failure to convert on third down will result in teams not scoring. Not only do they lose an opportunity to score, they also give their opponent an opportunity to put points on the board. Unquestionably, both their base, par down offense and their second-and-long offense will be key factors in determining how successful their offense will be. On the other hand, both of those offensive game situational elements, for the most part, often become set-ups for the all-important third-down offense situation. When they're successful, the two facets either produce a first down on their own or help create a relatively manageable third-down offense situation.

Conversely, when teams convert a third-down offense situation, they get a fresh set of downs to help them continue their effort to score. At a minimum, a successful conversion on third down is uplifting and intensely motivating. Furthermore, it can transform a very pressuring down situation into instant offensive momentum. In addition, allowing the offense to convert on third down can have an extremely negative and often disheartening impact on a defense. The aforementioned reasons are why many teams place more emphasis on their third-down offense than on any other facet of their offensive game planning. In fact, third-down offense is also a major consideration in the third and final major segment of total offensive game planning—red zone offense, which will be covered in Chapter 6.

Another key statistic that most teams feel impacts their likelihood of being successful is having the fewest number of three-and-outs. The attitude of most teams is, quite simply, that they are to rigorously avoid three-and-outs. They do not want their offense to experience three-and-outs. Three-and-outs take them off the field, stop their momentum, and give the football back to the opposition. And what is the most common culmination of a three-and-out series for the offense? A failed third-down offense conversion attempt.

Third-Down Offense Delineations

Third-down offense situations can be broken down into four categories. One is third-and-short, which involves third and one to two yards. Another is third-short-medium, which entails third and three to six yards. Yet another is third-and-medium-long, which is third and seven to nine yards. The final category is third-and-long, which is third and 10 yards or more. Figure 4-1 illustrates the four category delineations for third-down offense.

> • Third-and-short = third and one to two yards
> • Third-and-short-medium = third and three to six yards
> • Third-and-medium-long = third and seven to nine yards
> • Third-and-long = third and 10 yards or more

Figure 4-1. Third-down yardage delineations

Teams break down their third-down offense yardage situations into a variety of yardage-specific delineations for a number of reasons. In my case, I do so because I believe that many of the plays of my team's pass offense can produce the yardage needed to get a third-down conversion, which will, of course, produce a new first down. We have quickly timed play-action passes that will produce a sure two yards, if the ball is thrown to the first read, a running back in the flat. In a number of situations, those quick play-action passes can be employed on third-and-short situations, particularly when they incorporate a variety of formations, shifts, and motions to get different looks for the same plays. As we do with all play-action passes, we generally try to tie in to the runs we are planning to employ on third-and-short with the formations, shifts, and motions we also plan to use.

It is also important to note that the yardage parameters that teams establish for their third-down categories often can vary from team to team. For example, the third-and-short play call delineation for some teams is for one to three yards. In turn, a number of teams define a third-and-medium situation as being three to eight yards. Other programs consider third-and-long to be 9 to 12 yards and have a separate third-and-long situation that involves 13 yards or more. Whatever the delineations, the key is to have groupings of third down run and pass calls that, upon completion, should get the offense a first down. Personally, for example, I believe that my team can consistently get a nine-yard gain on our short, wide receiver comeback-out route. Ten yards? Perhaps. Truth be known, however, I'd rather not risk it. If I need 10 yards on third down, I'd rather make another play call that focuses on a pass route that *should* get that needed first-down yardage, rather than take such a risk with a short comeback-out route.

Another key factor that merits discussion at this point is that many teams will often employ route patterns on third-down situations in which they try to set up a shorter completion than the actual third-down yardage needed, provided that the play has the potential for the necessary run-after-the-catch yardage. For example, slant action, upon completion, is a route that often produces the critical extra yardage that results from the vertical run action of the receiver after the catch because of the upfield cut design of the slant. Although the slant route catch may be made only at five or six yards downfield, its run-action potential after the catch can often be the determining factor that secures the needed third-down yardage.

On third-down situations that involve longer yardage needs, teams have to assess their alternatives. For example, a 15-yard square-in route executed underneath a deep streak, clear-out route often allows the receiver to catch the ball and knife up the field for considerably greater yardage than the catch in itself.

One measure that coaches should never do is to ask a receiver to extend his route a set number of yards to allow him to achieve first-down yardage upon the reception. Pass-game precision is, in part, the result of proper timing of a pass route and the pass-throw action of the quarterback to a receiver who is executing a consistently run route. Coaches should never want an extended route assignment by a receiver. It's difficult enough to achieve well-timed accuracy between a quarterback and a receiver, let alone than to tell that receiver to deepen his route to obtain the required third-down yardage. If their teams need more yardage than a route is likely to get, coaches should call a deeper route pattern to produce the necessary yardage. Whatever the call and the circumstances, the receivers and the quarterback should always be put in a situation where they are attempting to execute a familiar route pattern that has been practiced over and over. As was noted previously, coaches also have the viable option to employ route patterns that offer the receiver a reasonable chance to run for the necessary third-down yardage after the reception. They also can run either a deep curl or a comeback-out route to gain the required yardage on a deep third-down yardage situation.

Manageable Third-Down Offense Yardage

A manageable third-down offense yardage situation is the basic goal of offensive coaches everywhere. They want either their base, par down offense or their second-and-long offense to put them in a third-and-short (one to two yards) or a third-and-short-medium (three to six yards) situation, at a maximum.

The underlying premise is that when in a manageable third-down offense yardage situation, their offense is in control. They firmly believe that something from their expansive pass-game arsenal can be utilized to effectively address a manageable third-down situation, whether it is play-action passing, quick-game passing, five- or seven-step timed dropback passing, roll-out or sprint-out passing, etc. Quickly timed play-action pass plays not only can lead to a easy quick throw for a first down, it also can provide an opportunity to hit a receiver down the field for a big gain. They also feel extremely confident that they can run the football in manageable third-down offense situations. Third and four? They might use one of their base run plays off of a formational design, possibly with shifts and motions that they think would be effective against their opponent's defense.

A manageable third-and-short or third-and-short-medium down situation enables the offense to be in control with regard to gaining the yardage needed on third down. On the other hand, when the offense needs to gain a minimum of nine yards on third down to get a first down, the advantage definitely falls to the defense. The biggest problem for the offense on third downs that have longer yardage needs is the time needed to protect the quarterback for longer pass-route throws.

Analyzing an Opponent's Third-Down Defense Tendencies

Much like their efforts to scrutinize their opponent's defensive efforts against their offense in base, par down offense situations, coaches initiate their work on their third-down offense game play call plan by analyzing breakdown videos of their next opponent's defense in third-down situations. As before, they analyze video footage of recent games that their opponent has recently played against teams that have offenses similar to theirs. Their evaluative efforts look at all of the defensive fronts, coverages, line games, stunts, and blitzes employed by their upcoming opponent in each of the third-down offense yardage situation delineations. As a result, each video breakdown analysis and study is specific to the various down-and-distance delineation categories (e.g., third-and-short, third-and-long, etc.).

One of the most effected play call, game-plan segments, when it comes to personnel plans, is the third-down offense determination. The underlying basis of this factor is that much like the offensive play call, game-plan efforts to utilize the very best play calls on third down, the defense often tries to do exactly the same. As a result, particular down offense situations that call for the utilization of specific offensive personnel will, likewise, often elicit the deployment of very specific defensive fronts and coverages to counter the personnel plans of the offense.

Creating a Third-and-Short Play Call Game Plan

As a rule, coaches initiate their efforts to devise a third-down offense play call game plan by addressing third-and-short (one to two yards) situations. For the offense, this factor is certainly extremely manageable. On the other hand, coaches also realize that the defense will be doing everything it can to "stuff" any attempt by the offense to gain the short yardage needed.

After an analysis of all of the third-and-short video clips that they have of their next opponent, coaches tend to be faced with certain questions. For example, what is their opponent's thinking for their third-and-short defensive efforts? Does the opponent load up its defensive front with special short-yardage fronts that can employ extra defensive linemen? Does the defense utilize a special short-yardage defensive front to combat a heavier run emphasis, such as a double eagle (Bear) type of defensive front? On the other hand, does the defense put forth base defensive fronts? Does the defense pressure with stunts and blitzes on third-and-short situations? Answers to these types of questions can enhance the level of understanding that coaches have of what actually are the problems that an opponent's third-and-short defense can present to them as they try to gain needed third-down short yardage.

With regard to their third-and-short offense, the initial part of the play call game plan that coaches should determine is their run game. They need to ask themselves how confident they are concerning whether they can muscle, or finesse, a first down with their run game. More importantly, they need to identify which run plays they think will work best against the short-yardage defenses they expect to encounter. No matter which running plays they select from their total run-game arsenal, it is highly likely that they will be simple, straight ahead run plays with little chance of incurring negative, or lost, yardage. On third-and-short situations, most coaches will avoid employing complicated blocking schemes that can be disturbed by defensive line stunts and blitzes. As such, more often than not in such a situation, they will utilize relatively non-complex plays, for example an inside or outside zone or, perhaps, an off-tackle power play. They may or may not run a sweep play, depending on whether or not the defense utilizes edge pressures on third-and-short situations. Even if the defense sometimes shows edge pressures on third-and-short situations, coaches still might run a sweep with the assistance of a wing-type blocker, in an effort to run the ball outside.

Depending on the circumstances, coaches might also consider using an option offense in third-and-short situations. For teams that utilize a run option offense, this viewpoint would be an excellent idea, particularly with the current widespread use of shotgun spread offense double- and triple-option read action. Run read options of any type tend to force a defense to become much more assignment-oriented, since a specific defender must be assigned to stop a triple-option's dive, quarterback keep, or pitch-action to a pitchback. Creating the need for a defensive assignment on option plays can often help to tame a pressuring, blitzing defense.

Some coaches might object to the possibility of employing an option offense on third-and-short yardage situations. As such, they might exclaim, "We're a great run counter team. Why would we want to eliminate our counter from our third-and-short run game attack thinking?" The straightforward answer to that is that they wouldn't and shouldn't. As noted previously, their basic key is to determine their best run plays that they believe they have in their third-and-short yardage play call list and run them. On the other hand, they need to determine which formations, with possible shifts and motions, can best help create advantages for those particular third-down run plays.

Coaches should also vary the cadences that they employ. Doing so may force the defense to jump offsides, which is a very easy way to get the yardage needed for a first down. This measure can occasionally work well, just as long as the offense is ready to execute and respond appropriately to such cadence variation.

Play-action passes can also be effective in third-and-short situations. Since running the football typically plays such a key role in third-and-short situations, a well-executed run fake can help to suck up linebackers and secondary defenders, thereby putting them out of position to cover receivers. Another key point to keep in mind is that coaches should be sure that they employ quickly timed play-action passes in these situations in order to help counter aggressive stunts and pressures that can be more threatening to longer-developing play-action passes.

One factor that most coaches like about possibly using quickly timed play-action passes in third-and-short situations is that a receiver might be left unguarded or poorly guarded. All factors considered, that pass-catcher might be the receiver who is working his route upfield to help produce an opportunity for a big yardage gain. Another key play-action pass alternative is to use bootlegs, naked bootlegs, and waggle play-action passes (with a pulling guard) on third-and-short situations. If this choice is adopted, the defense is confronted with defensing both play-action passing and counter-run-action.

Quick, three-step passing is another excellent way to get the needed yardage on third down. Not only does the offensive not have to block for very long, the quarterback can get his pass off quickly, which helps to better ensure a completion.

Roll-outs and sprint-outs can also be effective in third-and-short situations. Putting the quarterback out on the corner, with a run-pass option threat, is an excellent way to attack third-and-short defenses. On the other hand, employing sprint-out passing should not be an action that is a once-in-a-while play concept when converting a third-and-short yardage situation is the determining factor in whether or not an offense will keep possession of the ball when it's in the midst of a four-minute, eat-the-clock drive to win the game. Not surprisingly, coaches should not want to put the game on the line by calling a play, such as a sprint-out pass, if that play-action is rarely used or practiced.

The bottom line is that on third-and-short situations, coaches should use their best stuff, off of the formation and personnel plans that they feel provides them with the highest likelihood of succeeding. They should employ shifts and motions if they feel that a shift or motion will give them the best chance of succeeding. Figure 4-2 provides an example of a third-and-short game-plan, play call list.

THIRD-AND-SHORT

<u>RUNS</u>

ZOOM TWINS LT 47	ZOOM TWINS RT 46
STRONG RT TITE ZIN 12 BLAST	STRONG LT TITE ZIN 13 BLAST
ZOOM BUNCH LT SWEEP LT	ZOOM BUNCH RT SWEEP RT
SPLIT SLOT RT CRACK OPTION LT	SPLIT SLOT LT CRACK OPTION RT

<u>PASS</u>

ACE RT 90 HITCH	ACE LT 90 HITCH
ZOOM WING RT FAKE 22 FLOOD	ZOOM WING LT FAKE 23 FLOOD

Figure 4-2. An example of a third-and-short game-plan, play call list

Creating a Third-and-Short-Medium Play Call Game Plan

The next segment of a third-down offense play call game plan that coaches should address is third-and-short-medium (three to six yards). As discussed previously, for the offense, this situation can be a very manageable third down. In this circumstance, the offense is very much in control, whether it uses a run or a pass. All factors considered, the less yardage needed on a third-and-short-medium situation, the more a run play has credibility, with regard to gaining the required yards. As a rule, most of a team's base runs can still be employed effectively, particularly when utilized with formationing, shifts, and motions, and appropriate usage of personnel. This factor is especially applicable with simple, straight ahead run plays that can quickly crease the defense for sizeable chunks of yardage. Counters and reverse run plays can also be effective on third-and-short-medium yardage situations. Not only is the defense feeling the pressure of making a stop on the third-and-short-medium situation, it also has the added concern of having to legitimately worry about runs *and* passes. As a result, counters and reverses can often catch the third-down defense by surprise, given that it is typically focused on defending the more basic runs and passes.

Furthermore, run-option plays can be very effective on third-and-short-medium down yardage situations. A number of coaches whose teams employ a shotgun spread offense feel that their double- and triple-read option-actions are made for third-and-short-medium situations. This factor is particularly valid when the situation is third-and-three or third-and-four, since, all factors considered, a give to the dive/runningback on triple option-type plays will have a greater chance of successfully getting the needed yardage.

Depending on the ability of the offense to handle edge pressure, sweeps have also been found to be very effective in this situation. In addition, the use of draws will gain in favor, especially on deeper third-and-short-medium (five to six yards) situations that pose a greater threat of offensive pass-action.

As before, the offense is very much in control in extremely manageable third-and-short-medium situations. This factor is especially true in the pass game. For the most part, a pass completion should mean a first down. Coaches tend to be especially excited using quickly timed play-action passes that develop off of a realistic third-and-short-medium run-game threat. The quickness of execution helps to nullify the effectiveness of defensive stunts and blitzes on this particular third-down situation. The popularity of employing the quick-pass game on third-and-short-medium situations has merit. Not only can such quickly executed play-action passes enhance the ability to throw quickly, they also give the offense a realistic chance of gaining a first down, as well as the possibility of achieving an even more sizeable gain.

The quick-pass game can be an extremey viable course of action on third-and-short-medium situations. Coaches might have to be careful with hitches on a situation where six yards are needed for a first down. On the other hand, almost any completion in the quick-pass game will convert third-and-short-medium situations. Coaches especially like quick pass-game double-moves in third-and-short-medium situations, since the defensive secondary might aggressively jump an initial hitch, slant, or speed-out move, which could enable the second, double move, "go" portion of the route to pop open for a potential big gain. Of course, it could also result in an incompletion, which in turn would, most likely, lead to a punt and a subsequent loss-of-ball possession.

Sprint-out and even roll-out pass-action can be extremely effective on third-and-short-medium situations against perimeter pass defenders. The run-threat capabilities of the sprint-out quarterback in particular can place tremendous pressure on the secondary. Do they defend the pass and allow the quarterback to sprint for the first down? On the other hand, do the perimeter pass defenders defend the sprint-out run-action of the quarterback and leave receivers open to make first-down catches?

Bootleg, naked bootleg, and waggle pass-action can produce a similar run/pass threat to the defense's efforts to make a third-down stop. It is important to note, however, that such counter-pass action, especially naked bootlegs, can be very susceptible if the backside defensive end or linebacker rushes upfield.

Your dropback pass game can also be effective on third-and-short-medium situations. This factor is especially true on patterns with quick developing crossing routes that, in themselves, can produce the yardage needed for a first down upon completion. The main point of concern in this instance is the protection requirements for such longer developing routes. This reason is why the quick-pass game, sprint-out passes, quick play-action passes, and bootleg and naked run/pass action might better serve a team's very manageable third-and-short-medium yardage needs. Figure 4-3 offers an example of a third-and-short-medium game-plan, play call list.

THIRD-AND-SHORT-MEDIUM

<u>RUNS</u>

TREY RT 20 TRAP	TREY LT 21 TRAP
ZOOM I RT 34 LEAD DRAW	ZOOM I LT 33 LEAD DRAW
WING GUN SLOT RT 48 SHOVEL OPTION	WING GUN SLOT LT 49 SHOVEL OPTION
GUN SPREAD RT READ OPTION RT	GUN SPREAD LT READ OPTION LT
ACE RT 22/23 CHECK-WITH-ME	ACE LT 22/23 CHECK-WITH-ME

<u>PASS</u>

STRONG TWINS LT FAKE 23 FLOOD	STRONG TWINS RT FAKE 22 FLOOD
DOUBLE LT 90 SLANT	DOUBLE RT 90 SLANT
TREY RT 90 DOUBLE IN	TREY LT 90 DOUBLE IN
ZOOM DOUBLES LT 147 SMASH	ZOOM DOUBLE RT 247 SMASH
PRO RT 71 F DELAY	PRO LT 71 F DELAY
DOUBLES LT 145 Y CROSS	DOUBLES RT 245 Y CROSS

Figure 4-3. An example of a third-and-short-medium play call game plan

Creating a Third-and-Medium-
Long Play Call Game Plan

Addressing third-and-medium-long yardage needs (i.e., seven to nine yards) starts to expand beyond the attainable parameters of what constitutes a manageable third down. While seven to nine yards may certainly not seem insurmountable, a number of the very effective third-and-short and third-and-medium play call tools at the disposal of the play caller may no longer be appropriate. For example, other than draw plays or, perhaps, a quick trap play against a hard, upfield pass rush, runs simply don't look that inviting. Actually, some form of a quick-hitting dive or an inside-zone play could be utilized as a change of pace call in an effort to surprise a third-and-medium-long defense.

Another possibility on third-and-medium-long situations is using run-option plays, which can spring a pitch back free on the corner, particularly if a defense does not have a lot of experience defending run-option action. A lot of spread offense teams also feel quite comfortable utilizing double- and triple-option plays from a shotgun set on third-and-medium-long situations, especially if their quarterback is an excellent runner. Other than that, however, the run game has limited usage for third-down situations which require a seven to nine yard gain for a first down, unless the defense is, simply, overmatched.

From a pass-game standpoint, many of the play call weapons that can be effectively used in third-and-short yardage situations (one to two yards) and third-and-short-medium yardage situations (three to six yards) also dry up for the play caller when the third down becomes a third-and-medium-long (seven to nine yards) yardage situation. The quick-pass game, other than slants, runs out of gas at about six yards. Slants can get teams the needed seven to nine yards, because the slant receiver is on an upfield course when he makes the catch. His positioning and momentum gives him a good chance to continue upfield for the needed yardage.

Most other quick-game pass routes are, simply, not reliable enough to gain the needed seven to nine yards. The quick, short play-action passes that entail quick throws to the flat that are so effective in third-and-short and third-and-medium will, also, probably not get the needed yardage on a short-and-medium-long down situation. The same observations can also hold true for sprint-out passes, bootlegs, and waggles.

In reality, third-and-medium-long yardage situations (seven to nine yards) are not considered to be very manageable third-down situations. On the other hand, they are not thought of as unmanageable third-down situations either. As such, they are, simply, less manageable third-down situations that place greater obstacles on the offense's efforts to succeed. The main reason for this factor is that the threat of an effective running game has shrunken considerably, as has the possible effectiveness of the short-pass game. As a result, dropback pass action has to take on a greater role on third-and-medium-long yardage situations, which results in a less diversified offensive attack. As a consequence, the defense is confronted by fewer problems. In turn, less threats or problems provide the defense with a greater opportunity to target their focus on a much less-diversified offensive attack.

On the other hand, third-and-medium-long yardage situations (seven to nine yards) give the offense the advantage of being able to concentrate on its quicker and, most likely, shorter route patterns. To a substantial degree, patterns focusing on shorter and more quickly executed routes, such as short comeback-outs, option routes, short digs, cross routes, and other short isolation routes, enhance the likelihood that the offense will be able to protect the quarterback. This attribute is due to the lessened time needed for the quarterback to get those passes off.

More often than not, pass protection becomes the key factor on both third-and-medium-long and third-and-long yardage situations. As a rule, pass protection and blitz control are major concerns for third-and-medium-long passing situations. One of the advantages that a third-and-medium-long yardage down offers the offense is that vertical, anti-blitz sight adjustments and hot routes can effectively produce the yardage needed.

Straight dropback passing is certainly not the only passing means of attacking the defense on third-and-medium-long yardage situations. As such, moving the quarterback's launch point can be a key factor for the offense. If an offense only dropback passes on third-and-medium-long yardage situations, the defense is afforded an excellent opportunity to literally "tee off" on the quarterback's actual pass launch point. In that regard, roll-outs, sprint-outs, dashes, and designed scrambles can be excellent tools to help change the quarterback's pass launch point.

Play-action passes can also help offenses to gain the yardage they need on third-and-medium-long situations. The problem in this instance, however, is that play-action faking action will probably not have the same effect on the defense as it otherwise would on a base, par down offense situation or a third-and-short or a third-and-short-medium situation. On the other hand, some play-action passes can involve excellent maximum blocked protections, which enhance the time given to the quarterback to throw.

Maximum protections should be a major consideration when planning how to address third-and-medium-long yardage situations. This factor is especially true when third-down defenses become blitz oriented on third-and-medium-long and third-and-long yardage situations. One of the major problems for the offense, when it uses maximum protections, is that the offense may have definite problems getting all of its eligible receivers out into the designated pass pattern. Knowing that the defense a team is facing utilizes man coverage in this particular situation, whether they are blitzing or not, can, at a minimum, help the offense work three-man pattern route combinations. Such a concept is detailed in Figure 4-4.

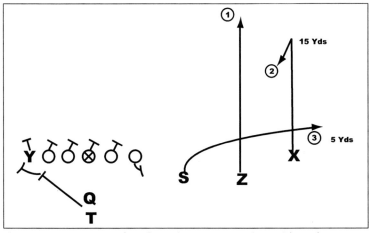

Figure 4-4. An example of maximum protection with a three-man route pattern

Screens and draws can also become a major factor in effectively addressing third-and-medium-long yardage situations. In these circumstances, the expectation of passes that the defense has can leave it vulnerable to draws, traps, and trapping draws. These plays can be very effective against up-the-field pass-pressuring defenses.

Shovel passes offer offenses an almost blend of a draw and a screen. Many shotgun spread offenses are quite competent at adding speed-option action to the shovel pass, as detailed in Figure 4-5.

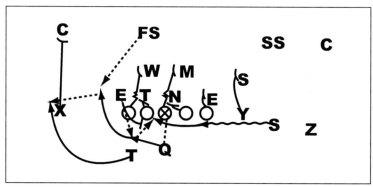

Figure 4-5. An example of the shotgun triple-option shovel pass

The screen world frequently comes alive on third-and-medium-long (seven to nine yard) situations. In this instance, the term "screen world" collectively refers to the great variety of screens being utilized by numerous teams, no matter what style of offense they employ. Back screens, wide-receiver screens, slot screens, and tight end screens are seemingly meshed into one, big screen package. Some of these screens can involve relatively slow, deliberate timing. Others act as speed screens, with the quarterback releasing his pass throw almost immediately upon receiving the center's snap. Other examples of screens include inside-middle screens and screens over the tackle-tight end area, in the alley between the furthest most offensive linemen and a wide receiver, or simply outside to a wide receiver. It could easily be argued that it is the variety of such screen plays with their mixture of personnel plans, formations, shifts, and motions, that makes these screen packages so effective and potentially such a vital weapon on third- and-medium-long yardage situations. Figure 4-6 provides an example of a third-and- long-medium play call game plan.

Creating a Third-and-Long Play Call Game Plan

A third-and-long (10 yards or more) situation is certainly not the manageable third-down yardage situation that coaches want. On third-and-long, the advantage is certainly slanted toward the defense. All factors considered, if the defense can contain deep pass threats and keep the football in front of them, it has an excellent chance of preventing the offense from converting situation into a first down, regardless of whether the pass is completed or not.

```
┌─────────────────────────────────────────────────────────────────────┐
│                      THIRD-AND-MEDIUM-LONG                            │
│                                                                       │
│                              RUNS                                     │
│                                                                       │
│  TREY RT 42 DRAW                      TREY LT 43 DRAW                  │
│  GUN SPREAD RT READ OPTION RT         GUN SPREAD LT READ OPTION LT     │
│                                                                       │
│                              PASS                                     │
│                                                                       │
│  WEAK RT 70 Y OPTION                  WEAK LT 70 Y OPTION              │
│  DBL SLOT LT 245 SLOT CROSS           DBL SLOT RT 145 SLOT CROSS       │
│  GUN TREY RT SPRINT RT ACUTES         GUN TREY LT SPRINT LT ACUTES     │
│  TREY RT 240 X COMEBACK               TREY LT 140 X COMEBACK           │
│  ACE RT 22 NAKED LT H BLOCK           ACE LT 23 NAKED RT H BLOCK       │
│  DOUBLES LT FAKE 22 FLOOD             DOUBLES RT FAKE 23 FLOOD         │
│  DOUBLES LT 146 HANK                  DOUBLES RT 246 HANK              │
│  TRIPS LT SOLID 146 CLEAR             TRIPS RT SOLID 246 CLEAR         │
│  TREY RT ROLL RT Z COMEBACK           TREY LT ROLL LT Z COMEBACK       │
│  TRIPS LT SWING SCREEN LT             TRIPS RT SWING SCREEN RT         │
└─────────────────────────────────────────────────────────────────────┘
```

Figure 4-6. An example of a third-and-long-medium play call game plan

Deep, prevent zone defenses can help shut down deep-pass route combinations. Combination zone and man-to-man coverages, such as two-man under coverage or man-free coverage can effectively allow for deep-zone coverage, with tight, underneath man-to-man coverage. If the defense feels its secondary-coverage defenders are superior to their opponent's offensive receivers, it may, simply, attempt to shut down the pass game with one-on-one man coverage concepts. Furthermore, since many deeper route combinations can take a longer time to develop, blitz pressure is often afforded more time to execute its stunts and blitzes.

All of the aforementioned factors concepts can easily create a relatively bleak picture for the offense, with regard to its effort to convert third-and-long situations. Although third-and-long down yardage situations are not categorized as manageable third-down situations, the offense needs to believe that it *can* convert third-and-long yardage down situations. In addition, the offense must realize that the degree to which it is able to succeed in its efforts to convert these situations may very well affect the final outcome of the game. Unfortunately, too many coaches hold an attitude that third-and-long down yardage situations *will not* be converted and a that a fourth-down punt is inevitable.

Such a negative attitude, in itself, is almost enough to eliminate any possibility of success on third-and-long down yardage situations. In reality, the opposite attitude *must* be held. In fact, both coaches and players must be confident in their belief that they can, and will, be effective in their efforts to attack third-and-long situations. While teams may not consistently achieve the same level of conversion success that they do on third-and-short, third-and-short-medium, or even third-and-medium-long yardage situations, they *can* be relatively effective on critical third-and-long yardage down situations through hard work and effort, focus, game planning, and concentrated practice.

The initial area of concern for our third-and-long down yardage play call game planning is pass protection. In that regard, coaches have to address a number of issues. For example, are they going to face a base rush of defensive linemen, with maximum or near maximum pass-drop coverage? Are they going to see frontal stunts and/or secondary-blitz pressure, with man and/or zone coverage behind such defensive pressure? Furthermore, are they going to see a mixture of such concepts?

If they are going to be confronted by base defensive line pass rush action involving three or four defensive linemen and/or outside linebackers, they should then focus on attacking the pass coverages they expected to see, based on their video breakdown analyses. On the other hand, if they are expecting to face heavy blitz pressure, then maximum or, at least, extra protection must be one of their first considerations.

More often than not, much of the basis for a team's approach to providing maximum pass protection on third-and-long situations is derived from the realization that many of its pass-game blitz controls (e.g., sight-adjustment routes, hot and warm routes, and routes designated as blitz-beater routes within a pass pattern) do not work very effectively for addressing long-yardage situation needs. For example, while a sight-adjustment route or a hot or warm throw might net a team eight, nine, or ten yards. However, if the yardage to be gained on third down is 12 or 13 yards, the defense may, very well, be able to bait the offense to throw to such a blitz-control route to purposely force the offense to come up short of the yardage it needs for a first down.

If coaches feel that they need maximum protection, their initial thought should be to utilize seven-man protections employing either five offensive linemen and two backs or five offensive linemen, one tight end, and one back. These two, maximum seven-man protections are illustrated in Figures 4-7 and 4-8.

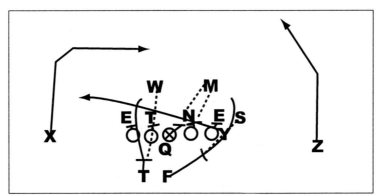

Figure 4-7. An example of seven-man protection, with five offensive linemen and two backs

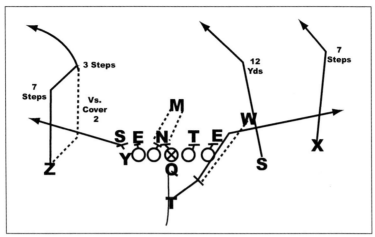

Figure 4-8. An example of seven-man protection, with five offensive linemen, a tight end, and one back

Maximum seven-man protection does not necessarily mean that the tight end and one back or the two backs have to stay in to block. As such, they can be assigned single-man protection targets or two targets, such as when a back checks an inside linebacker to an outside linebacker or a strong safety-type defender. A back could also be assigned two zone areas to block, such as the "C" to "D" gap, from the inside to the outside of the block of a tight end, as was shown in Figure 4-4. In either case, the tight end or backs could be given block-check release assignments. In this instance, the blocker would stay in to block if, in his man or zone blocking assignment, the assigned defender pass rushes. He would release into a pass route if his assigned defender doesn't pass rush.

Using a tight end to block, check-release helps to elongate the corner for end-of-line rushers. In reality, the same factor can be true when a tight end releases into a pass route from his normal, on-the-line-of-scrimmage alignment. One negative aspect of utilizing a tight end blocker is that he can be of little use blocking if the defender he is assigned to block does not rush due to the tight end's on-the-line-of-scrimmage alignment. Two blocking backs can be of double help in picking up, or helping on, free, unblocked rushers late, after they have checked their own assigned blocking targets. On the other hand, without a tightly aligned tight end, a maximum protection seven-man blocking scheme, with two backs in the backfield, can be negatively affected by having to contend with the outside rush of two defenders off of two short corners.

Figure 4-9 provides an example of maximum two-back, seven-man blocking protection. Both backs man-protection block-check the inside to the outside linebacker/strong safety-type defender to their sides. If neither of those defenders rush, each back is free to check for an extra outside rusher to the opposite side. This action is not as difficult a task as it may seem. From their backfield alignments, especially if from a two-point, upright stance, it is relatively easy for the backs to see the tilted man or zone coverages roll to the side of such pressure before the snap of the football.

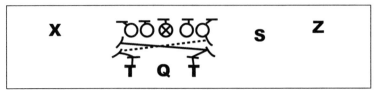

Figure 4-9. An example of maximum two-back, seven-man blocking protection

One other protection factor that can be utilized with maximum protection schemes, or any other pass protection type scheme, is the concept of having the backfield pass-protection blockers "chip out." Chipping out involves the backfield pass-protection assignment of helping to assist the block of the offensive tackle to the side of the back's pass-route release. In the simplest of terms, if an offensive back checks his blocking assignment and sees that his blocking assignment is dropping off into pass coverage, he is given the added assignment of helping the offensive tackle to his side block the pass rusher that the tackle is attempting to block. Chipping out is a rip-through technique through the outside half of the defender if the back sees that the tackle is losing, or beginning to lose, his block on the pass rusher.

In this instance, the back simply rips through the outside of the pass rusher, using low-pad control to slow down the pass rusher's efforts to beat the offensive tackle to the outside before the back continues on into his assigned pass route. If the offensive tackle is in control of the defender he is blocking, the back forgets the chip-out action and just continues on into his assigned pass route. The basic rule is, if the back sees a lot of "color" from the pass rusher's uniform, he rips through such color and then works into his assigned pass route.

In reality, the approach of coaches with regard to third-and-long pass-route patterns should be altered to address the problems that the defense could present while trying to avoid giving the yardage needed by the offense to earn a first down. A good starting point concerning how to gain deeper yardage on third-down situations is to analyze the opponent's defense on third downs to determine what type of one-on-one or two-on-one deep streak, post, and post-corner route isolations the offense can devise against the third-and-long coverages of the defense.

Much of the effort to identify favorable pass route and pattern isolations focuses, once again, on the use of varied personnel plans, formationing, shifts, and motions. One key issue in this regard is whether the use of a specific formation or motion can produce a one-one-one streak isolation against a particular cornerback. Versus a two-deep, open-middle coverage, a three-on-two deep streak isolation could be utilized. Against a three-deep, closed-middle coverage, a team could employ a four-vertical pass concept to produce a two-on-one deep streak isolation on the middle free safety.

The same factor can be true with post and double-post route combinations. Outside post-corner routes can also lead to such deep one-on-one isolations, as can a post/post-corner scissors route combination, as illustrated in Figure 4-10.

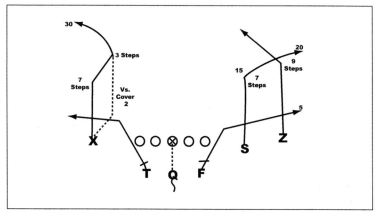

Figure 4-10. An example of a deep post-post corner scissors route combination

Another third-down-and-long deep-route combination that can be very effective is a deep streak or post clear-out, with a deep cross or dig route underneath such clear-out action. Figure 4-11 provides an example of a deep streak, clear-out route, with a deep dig inside-crossing route, working underneath such clear-out action. Figure 4-12 illustrates a deep post, clear-out route, with an across-the-field deep cross route, working underneath such clear-out action.

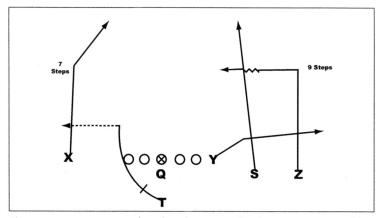

Figure 4-11. An example of a deep streak, clear-out route, with a deep underneath dig route

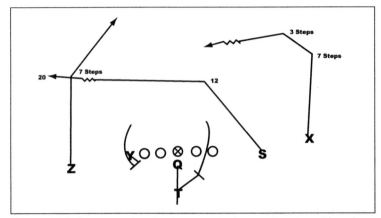

Figure 4-12. An example of a deep post, clear-out route, with a deep underneath cross route

It should be noted that deep high-low, read route combinations can effectively suck up a cornerback or a safety, thereby enhancing the effort to gain the yardage needed on such third-down situations. Subsequently, a pass can be thrown over the top of such a defender, as illustrated in Figures 4-13 and 4-14. Figure 4-13 illustrates a deep smash, high-low read concept, with the low route at 12 yards. The deeper low route is based on the premise of influencing the cornerback to jump the low route so that the deep, over-the-top route can be open for the big-yardage completion. Figure 4-14 details a similar deep, high-low read, only to the inside. Some teams refer to this combination as the "fish" concept with the low, 12-yard stop route serving as the bait for the safety to jump up on, with the deep, over-the-top post route constituting as the fishing pole to be thrown deep, if the safety does jump up on "the bait."

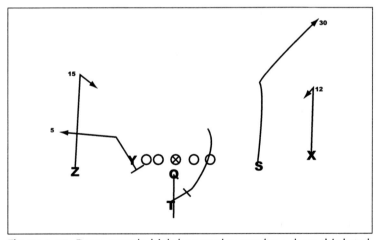

Figure 4-13. Deep smash, high-low read to produce deep third-and-long yardage

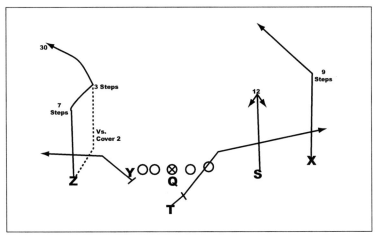

Figure 4-14. Deep fish, high-low read to produce deep third-and-long yardage

Such deep, vertical stretch routes are not always required to get the needed third-and-long yardage. It should be remembered that "third-and-long" means "third-and 10 yards or more." As such, a deep streak route may not necessarily be needed to get the required 10, 11, or 12 yards to convert such a third-down situation. A 15-yard curl route or an 18 to 15 yard deep comeback-out route can definitely attain such shorter third-and-long yardage needs. By the same token, shorter, 10-yard type square-in or square-out routes can allow for catches that enable the receiver to knife up the field for additional run yardage after the catch. The same factor can hold true for such routes as 10- to 12-yard speed-outs, whether they are outside wide-receiver isolation routes or isolation routes that break underneath streak clear-outs. Even slant isolation routes can effectively address a team's third-and-long yardage needs, since the slant receiver has a relatively good chance of gaining sufficient extra yardage after the catch, so long as the needed yardage is not too great. In addition, draws and screens are still extremely viable possibilities.

As can be seen, third-and-long offense requires very special game planning, protections, and play call needs. It certainly is a difficult critical-offensive situation. Although it is not the manageable third-down offense situation that teams strive for on downs, it is *not* an insurmountable game situation. Accordingly, coaches need to make their third-and-long offense a priority, a *top* priority, during the off season, preseason, and in-season, in regard to their efforts for game and practice planning. If they do, they may be pleasantly surprised with regard to the level of success that their team experiences in its seasonal third-down-and-long conversion efforts.

Practice Planning Tuesday's Play Call Game Plans

Hypothetically, it's Tuesday morning. It's now time for the coaching staff to get to work on planning their Tuesday afternoon practice. They have accomplished their goal of creating their base, par down offense situation game plan, as well as their second-and-long situation game plan. In addition, they completed their third-down offense situation game plan by the time they left work to head home on Monday evening. At this point, they need to sit down and develop their individual, unit, and team offensive practice-plan work so that they can start to be ready to execute their total play call game plan come game time.

Planning Off of a Daily Master Practice Plan

The key to sound practice planning is to plan off of a constant, well-conceived master daily practice schedule. Such a master daily practice schedule is usually set up either by the head coach, his three coordinators (offensive, defensive, and special teams), or by a meeting of all four of those coaches. A master daily practice schedule can be set up in a number of ways. One option is to plan around a two-hour (24, five-minute periods) practice schedule. Such a schedule would not include either stretching or post-practice conditioning. An example of a blank master daily practice schedule is provided in Figure 5-1.

Date:		Day:		Time:	
Pre-Practice:					
Period	**WR**	**QB**	**RB**	**TE**	**OL**
1					
2					
3					
4					
5					
6					
7					
8					
9					
10					
11					
12					
13					
14					
15					
16					
17					
18					
19					
20					
21					
22					
23					
24					

Figure 5-1. An example of a blank master daily practice schedule

In reality, coaches who adhere to the aforementioned schedule may rarely utilize 24 periods of practice during the season. On the other hand, they might use all 24 during spring practice when they are attempting to maximize as much individual-position practice drilling as possible. During the season, however, they may be more apt to use 21 periods of practice, or less, rather than the full 24. Even with 21 periods of practice for a total of one hour and 45 minutes, they will still find themselves on the practice field for over two hours, when all of the pre-practice stretching, warm-up, and post-practice conditioning are added to the total.

When planning, most coaches want to be on the practice field for a maximum time of two hours. Unfortunately, that objective can often be difficult to accomplish on a team's two heavy game-week practice days, Tuesday and Wednesday. Any excess time devoted to practice on Tuesday and Wednesday is averaged out over the course of the week, as a game week winds down. For example, Thursday may customarily be a lighter practice day, involving only 15 periods for a total of one hour and 15 minutes. Friday traditionally encompasses a nine-period practice for a total of 45 minutes. Furthermore, when a team has travelling constraints, they might not go out on the practice field at all. Instead, they might have a walk-through drill somewhere at the hotel at which the team is staying.

As the season wears on, most teams tend to start to pare down their total number of practice periods in an effort to keep their team as fresh as possible come game day. Coaches should adhere to one foremost rule. If they feel that their team seems to be getting tired and/or a bit stale, they should cut back. As was noted previously, no substitute exists for freshness. The primary area in which coaches often try to physically cut back the most is on their heavy Tuesday and Wednesday practices.

Planning Tuesday's Unit and Team Practice Periods

At this point, either the head coach, his coordinators (offensive, defensive, and special teams), or all four of those coaches must determine which periods are going to be used for offensive/defensive work against each other and which periods are to be designated as team periods, working against scout squads. The effort is undertaken by identifying an overall base practice-plan structure that details how they plan their walk-through drills, their special team's drills, their individual drills, their unit drills (e.g., a 7-on-7 skeleton pass drill) and their team drills.

Their efforts to develop their practice plan structure (for a 21-period practice) may start by assigning periods #1 and #2 as collectively a 10-miniute interval for walk-through drills. Periods #3 to #5 are designated for special teams practice for 15 minutes. Periods #6 to #9 are allotted a 20-minute segment for individual position skills practice. Periods #10 to #13 are allocated 20 minutes for unit practice. Periods #14 to #15 are assigned 10 minutes for either unit or team drills, thereby providing a considerable degree of flexibility for coaches to work on whichever aspect would best suit their needs for that particular practice. Periods #16 through #21 are given 30 minutes for team practice, usually against the scout squad, which emulates the defense of that week's opponent. It should be noted that the two periods that have been allotted a 10-minute session for either an extra unit or team practice helps give coaches a great deal of flexibility to address their particular practice needs. An example of an overall preliminary practice-plan structure is illustrated in Figure 5-2.

It should be noted that the overall practice-plan structure detailed in Figure 5-2 is a "base" plan. The base plan encompasses a very structured plan that progresses from

Date:		Day:		Time:	
Pre-Practice:					
Period	**WR**	**QB**	**RB**	**TE**	**OL**
1			Walk-Through Drills		
2					
3			Special Teams Drills		
4					
5					
6			Individual Position Skills Drills		
7					
8					
9					
10			Unit Drills		
11					
12					
13					
14			Unit or Team Drills		
15					
16			Team Drills		
17					
18					
19					
20					
21					

Figure 5-2. An example of an overall preliminary practice-plan structure

walk-throughs (activities in which coaches get to truly teach any new concepts or put in extra coaching and teaching emphasis on plays that need cleaning up) to special teams to individual position drills to unit drills to team drills. More often than not, most coaches purposely don't adhere to a strict progression of walk-through drills to special teams drills to individual drills to unit drills to team drills.

Undoubtedly, every coach, at one time or another, has seen football practices where both the players and the coaches seem to run around the field like a bunch of robots, programmed to go automatically go from drill to drill. While a practice plan structure can progress from walk-through teaching to individual to unit to team drills, a football game never follows such a rigid, structured progression. For example, a team may have its offense fail to convert on a third-down play, punt the football away, see the punt returner drop the punt, and have the ball recovered by its punt coverage team. Its offense, which just came off the field having experienced failure, subsequently finds itself back on the field, with a fresh new set of downs in excellent field position to score.

On one hand, an offense could find itself in a critical coming-out offense situation, on the minus one-yard line and one or two plays later, could be confronted by circumstances in which it is in a critical goal-line offense situation, on the plus one-yard line going in. Without question, a football practice can be highly structured to go from an individual to a unit to a team emphasis. On the other hand, jumping around from one teaching and coaching concept to another distinctly different teaching and coaching concept during the course of practice can be very productive. In fact, such a practice procedure could be extremely valuable in helping *all* of a team's players to develop a solid sense of mental and physical flexibility that a wild and wooly 60-minute football game normally demands.

Figure 5-3 details an example of an overall base daily practice-plan structure for a heavy Tuesday practice day. As can be seen, the offense's practice emphasis on Tuesday is base, par down offense, second-and-long offense, and third-down offense. The plan, for the most part, follows the team's overall base daily practice-plan structure. It has the same ratio of practice period-type allotments as the overall base daily practice-plan structure shown in Figure 5-2. It even displays how the team allows for practicing with flexibility by having an extra unit period for a unit, inside-run drill periods #7 and #8, instead of having eight team periods.

It should be noted that some sense of practice flexibility exists with the varied orderings of the individual, unit, and team drills that make up the specific practice structure for a particular day. More often than not, such drill order variation is undertaken for specific reasons. One major reason for such variation in the example shown in the overall, base Tuesday practice-plan schedule is to interject some lighter, non-contact type drills in between the long series of more physical drills. This step is undertaken in an attempt to try and prevent the players from getting overly fatigued, and, as a result, possibly injured due to long sessions of heavy-hitting drills.

A review of the overall preliminary practice-plan structure detailed in Figure 5-3 shows the start of practice (periods #1 and #2) having a two-period teaching and coaching walk-through period for ten minutes. Whether the walk-through period is focused on the offense's run game, pass game, or both, the walk-through period provides for on-the-field meetings, in which a virtual walking-through specific assignments and techniques is the method of focusing in on verbal teaching and coaching from the coach. The same information could also be given to the players in a classroom setting. It should be noted, however, that sitting in a chair, listening to the coach's informational presentation, is simply not the same as having those same players physically walk-through through the coach's targeted message. To walk-through their assignments correctly, the players have to focus in on the coach's teaching and coaching words.

Date:		Day:		Time:	
Pre-Practice:					
Period	**WR**	**QB**	**RB**	**TE**	**OL**
1	Walk-Through Drills				
2					
3	Special Teams Drills				
4					
5	Individual Run	Individual Run	Individual Run	Individual Run	Individual Run
6					
7	Wide Receivers vs. Cornerbacks	Unit Inside Run Drill			
8					
9	Individual Pass	Individual Pass	Individual Pass	Individual Pass	Individual Pass
10					
11	Unit 1-on-1 Pass Drill				1-on-1 Pass Pro vs. Def.
12					Twist Pass Pass Pro vs. Def
13	Unit 7-on-7 Skeleton Pass Third Down Drill vs. Scouts				
14					
15	Special Teams				
16	Team Base, Par Down Offense vs. Scouts				
17					
18	Team Second-and-Long Offense vs. Scouts				
19	Team Third Down Offense vs. Scouts				
20					
21					

Figure 5-3. An example of an overall base Tuesday practice-plan structure

Periods #3 and #4, which are allotted a 10-minute period, are devoted to practicing special teams games. If coaches don't have a specific reason for interjecting practice for their special teams during other parts of their practice, they should strongly consider putting special teams right near the top of their practice schedule to highlight its importance. Such a measure helps to stress special teams play—"first and foremost." Accordingly, more often than not, after their walk-through drills, the first full-speed drill practice-action of most teams can be special teams work.

Furthermore, teams generally find that scheduling the practice of their special teams can provide them with a good opportunity to break up having too many offensive and defensive drills in a row. In fact, special teams work can fit into the beginning, middle, or end of practice, just as it can occur in the beginning, middle, or end of the game at any time. As a result, many teams like to interject their special teams practice at different stages, all throughout practice, on an almost daily basis. Not only can doing to help infuse variety into practice, it can also help prevent the mood associated with a boring, stale practice. It should be noted, for example, that the third planned special teams practice period for the practice-plan schedule detailed in Figure 5-3 is scheduled during Period #15. This particular ordering of practice is designed to separate the physically demanding individual and unit run and pass-protection drills and the six periods of challenging physical team drills.

After two periods of individual run practice drills (periods #5 and #6), the unit, 9-on-7 inside run drill (periods #7 and #8) is employed by many teams as one of the key, physical drills that they use to get their base, par down run-game ready for their upcoming opponent this week. Although a physical drill, the drill is executed in a thud (non-scrimmage/non-tackling) context. This unit drill period can be utilized as the optional unit or team run period, which provides a team with six unit practice periods for the day. Although this drill could not be employed against scout-squad players, most teams execute the drill by pitting the first-team offense against the first-team defense. Some programs pit their first-team offense against their second-team defense and then switch for the second round of repetitions.

As a rule, in this drill, the offensive and defensive coordinators work together scripting the drill so that each side of the football will be able to work against defensive looks and offensive plays that are relatively close to what will be employed by this week's upcoming opponent. In some instances, the defensive coordinator may go so far as to use some pre-planned defensive fronts, stunts, or blitzes off of drawn cards in order to help the offense. Likewise, the offensive coordinator might utilize some specific plays, not in his own offensive repertoire, to specifically help the defense prepare against such run plays for the upcoming week's opponent. A depiction of the unit, 9-on-7 inside-run drill is outlined in Figure 5-4. (Note that the dotted S's are shown in Figure 5-4 to denote safeties.) Most defensive coaches prefer having their safeties practice in the 9-on-7 inside-run drill, but not in a live context, since there are no wide receivers in the drill to block them. As a result, the safeties are in the drill to practice their gap run fits. The safeties do so by taking two, or three steps to the ball carrier's run path and then breaking down into a tackling position only.

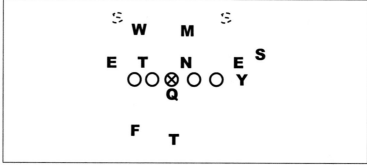

Figure 5-4. An example of a unit, 9-on-7 inside-run drill

While the 9-on-7 inside-run drill is being executed, the wide receivers and cornerbacks work together in some type of unit drill. Figure 5-5 illustrates both groups working together in a unit, 1-on-1, wide receiver/cornerback block drill.

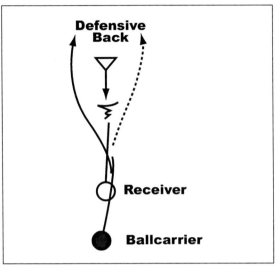

Figure 5-5. An example of a unit, 1-on-1, wide receiver/cornerback block drill

Periods #9 and #10 are two more segments that are often assigned as individual coaching periods for the teaching, coaching, drilling, and practicing of the individual-position skills and techniques. Given that two segments of individual coaching periods have already been utilized for the run game, at this point, these two additional individual periods are for the teaching, coaching, and practicing of pass-game skills and techniques. Furthermore, just as they did with the run-game, coaches begin their efforts to work on the pass-game in a most basic form—by practicing the skills and techniques with individual practice periods. Figure 5-3 depicts the two individual pass-emphasis intervals (Periods #9 and #10), leading into the unit 1-on-1, pass drill segments (periods #11 and #12). Simultaneously, the offensive line engages in a unit, 1-on-1, pass pro drill with the defensive line. Then, the unit, 7-on-7, third-down offense skeleton pass drill phases (periods #13 and #14) are conducted. Concurrently, the offensive line practices against the defensive line in a unit, twist, pass pro, pick-up drill.

It is important to note that since one of the key practice-plan concepts for Tuesday is third-down offense, the unit, 7-on-7, skeleton pass drill is built around third-down offense situations. Furthermore, by using rapid-fire, first team-second team, first team-second team repetitions against the defense, coaches are able to get a minimum of eight repetitions in a five-minute period. As a result, on a two-period unit, 7-on-7, third-down offense, skeleton pass drill, the coaches can be confident that 16 repetitions can be performed.

The down situation can vary, according to the wishes of the coaches. For example, the first four repetitions might be a third-and-four down situation. The second set of four repetitions might be second-and-six. The third group of four repetitions might be third-and-eight. The final four repetitions might be third-and-thirteen. The key point is that on Tuesday, third-down situation considerations, most coaches will usually slightly adjust the yardage needs every time a unit, 7-on-7, skeleton pass drill is conducted.

As was previously discussed, period #15 depicts a special teams practice insertion, if only for five minutes. Having the special teams run on the field for a last-minute, field-goal attempt and/or field-goal block can be an effective way to utilize a shorter block of special teams practice time. As stated earlier, interjecting a special teams period in the middle of a practice can help add variety to practice and can help break up a daily practice plan that is often the same, or almost the same, every day. Another approach for coaches is to have the special teams practice the last three periods of their scheduled practice time, as a way to culminate practice, imbedding an attitude of "saving the best for last."

Periods #16 to #21 (collectively, 30 minutes of practice time) are what all previous individual and unit drills and practice work build up to—the team periods versus the scout squad. Figure 5-3 shows that the focus of the team periods is whatever key game-planning concepts have been targeted for the day, for example, base, par down offense, second-and-long offense, and third-down offense. At this point, coaches work hard on their play call scripting and their scripting of what they believe their opponent will do to defense them in each critical game situation. Every effort is made to enact practice that is as game-like as possible, with regard to what coaches expect to see come game-day against their opponent.

It is important to remember that teams are not locked into the overall base daily practice plan structure, an example of which is presented in Figure 5-3. A daily practice plan is a tool that coaches employ to help their offense prepare for their opponent of the week. In reality, they can make whatever changes that they feel that they need to make to maximize the effectiveness of their daily practice plan structure work for them and their offense.

If the next opponent of a coach is an excellent blitz team, he might definitely look for ways to "steal" extra practice time from somewhere in his daily practice plan structure for an extra team blitz pick-up drill. On the other hand, he might feel he needs extra practice time to prepare to face his opponent's 3-3 stack defense, which no one else on his schedule utilizes. "What could I possibly eliminate from practice to put in an extra team, blitz pick-up drill?" he might ask. "Cut out the unit, one-on-one drill?" That drill involves a pretty important route versus man-coverage skills to consider omitting. "How about eliminating the walk-through drill?" One way or the other, he has to make such decisions on a weekly, and even a daily, basis. That determination is the only way to help provide his offense with enough practice flexibility to best help his offense to be properly prepared to excel against their next opponent.

Put Tuesday's Play Call Game Plan on Boards in the Staff Room

Once any of the specific play call game plans have been determined (e.g., the third-down offense or the red zone offense), coaches immediately put the actual play call game-plan lists on blank charts on the grease boards in their offensive staff room. For example, as a result, all third-down offense or red zone offense play calls are listed in total (with personnel plans, formations, shifts, and motions) on both the left and right side of the charts to denote left- and right-hash mark calls. If coaches plan to only attempt to execute a specific run or a pass from the middle of the field, they would list the play in the middle of the play call card to indicate such middle-of-the-field-only usage. Run plays are listed first, while pass plays of any kind are posted second, separated by a dotted line.

On staffs, a graduate assistant coach is usually responsible for copying the play call lists onto the actual game, play call chart that is shown on a computer, as the game-plan, play call lists are created on the offensive staff-room boards. Depending on the situation, a manager could be assigned to do such typing or a member of the student body at large could be solicited to type the weekly game-plan play list off of the grease boards in the offensive room to a computer game-plan, play list system. Doing so could earn that individual a manager's letter in recognition of such valuable seasonal work.

Once the game-plan play calls have been written on the offensive staff room boards, coaches consider those plays as the initial draft of their specific situational play call needs. After each practice, coaches will analyze their initial game-plan, play call decisions to see which ones they like best and which should be eliminated, given their ineffectiveness as demonstrated by an evaluation of practice video footage after each practice session.

Whenever specific play is eliminated with its particular personnel plan, formation, and possible shift or motion, the play is not erased off the board. Instead, a red line is drawn through the play that's being eliminated. As a consequence, coaches are able to see what has been eliminated from their game-plan, play call sheet, which helps them determine if a hole (need) has been created in that particular plan by doing so. In fact, on any number of occasions, coaches may eliminate a particular play after a Tuesday practice, only to add it back after a Wednesday or even a Thursday practice to fill a particular need that might have been forged when the play was initially dropped from the game-plan, play call list.

Having the situational game-plan, play call lists on the boards in the staff room helps to visually produce a big picture of the plan for every coach in the room to see. Subsequently, as the game-plan, play call list grows from day to day, the coaches are able to make personal, constructive analyses throughout the process of developing the offensive game plan. One coach, for example, may see a need for more diversification concerning the use of a particular run or pass play, given the fact that it is listed on a large number of play call situations. Another coach may call for the elimination of a particular play for a specific play call situation. On the other hand, the same coach may offer an excellent idea regarding how that same play could be employed for a totally different play call situation.

It should be noted that some coaches simply determine which plays they want for specific play call down situations, type the decisions into the computer, and erase the listing of those plays from off the offensive staff room's board. Personally, I want my offensive staff's game-plan thinking to grow during the course of the game week, just as the actual offensive game plan evolves and develops over the same span of time.

Once coaches have determined what run and pass plays they want to utilize, they have to decide *how* they're going to order the particular game-situation, game-plan play calls. Some coaches number the preference of the play calls from top to bottom. Others designate their preferred play call for each particular game-plan situation and then simply group the rest of the situational play calls together by the type of personnel plans, formations, shifts, and motions utilized.

In reality, some coaches believe in only having a few possible play calls per play call situation. As a result, on third-and-short, they might only have two run calls and one play-action pass or one quick, three-step, timed pass. The value of having a short play call list plan for each particular play call situation is that a small number of such play call possibilities generally does not require a substantial amount of practice time and practice repetitions to prepare a team to effectively execute those potential situational play calls. Other coaches prefer to have a quantitatively larger of number of plays for each play call situation. As such, every coach has to decide for himself.

Personally, I don't like to be limited by a small number plays, just in case those particular plays, or styles of plays, don't seem to be working well at a critical point in time of a game. I prefer to have a bit larger of a situational game-plan, play call list, with differing styles of plays, utilizing a variety of personnel plans, forms, shifts, and motions. As a result, I rarely seem to feel stuck for a play call when I certainly don't need or want to feel stuck.

In response to my approach to this factor, some coaches might exclaim, "That means more practice time is needed for each situational play call need. I don't know where we'll find the time to get all that done." In reality, as a season goes on or as their program, in general, matures, they will often find that they will utilize certain types, or packages, of plays for particular game situations. Accordingly, they will discover that they practice those plays in many or at least a number of other game-plan situational needs. While they might run a particular play over and over during the course of a game, when they disguise a particular play with mixed personnel plans, formations, shifts, and motions usage, a play can be called over and over again without the defense having good read keys to actually know what particular play is going to be run. Furthermore, all factors considered, running a play over and over can help develop a familiarity of execution that can help to make a play consistently successful.

Over the years, at the end of a season, many coaches make it a point to thoroughly analyze and study their situational game-plan, play call lists. In reality, it can be surprising to some individuals how quantitatively small each grouping of situational play calls are. More often than not, it is the variety of personnel plans, formations, shifts, and motions that seem to establish the perception of the variety and quantity, not the actual number of play calls themselves. As a rule, most coaches find that for each game-plan, play call situation, they seem to use a rather small number of plays over and over. The perception of having variety in the play calls is derived from the differing personnel plans, formations, shifts, and motions.

The aforementioned doesn't mean that coaches will employ certain plays only once or twice in a particular grouping of play calls, because they certainly will. What it does mean is that the list of often-used plays in particular game-plan, play call situations will be somewhat limited because of the play call parameters each situation may impose on the decision whether or not to use a particular play. If their team is in the red zone on the 12-yard line, coaches are probably not going to call a deep pass. If their opponent's red zone defense blitzes on every down, the chances are relatively good that they're not going to call play-action pass plays that require a lot of protection time in order for the quarterback to get his pass off. Such decision-making parameters, in themselves, will often limit the type of play calls coaches can or cannot, and should or should not, make.

Creating Tuesday's Practice-Period Scripts

A team's practice-period scripts set up a list, or order, of plays coaches want to work on in the limited amount of time that they have to practice certain pre-determined, game-like situations. Periods #16 and #17 in Figure 5-3, for example, have been assigned to practice team base, par down offense. In this scenario, the underlying premise is that coaches should be able to work on 14 scripted plays in the two-period, 10-minute block of scheduled practice time.

On Tuesdays, for hash mark considerations, many coaches start out by assigning the first two plays to the left hash, a play in left-center, one play in the middle of the field, one play in right-center, and then two plays on the right hash. This progression gives them a seven-play sequence, going from left to right. On the next seven plays, they reverse the order, with the first two plays on the right hash, a play in right-center, one play in the middle of the field, a play in left-center, and finally two on the left hash. This progression has them practicing four straight plays in a row on the right hash, as a result of the second seven-play progression that takes them from right to left.

Coaches can adhere to this practice football-field alignment ratio so that their offense gets a variety of field-position practice, not just working on the hash marks or in the middle of the field. If they scheduled a three-period block of practice time, they would then have a third set of starting points to practice from a variety of field positions, beginning from the left hash and working from left to right again.

Figure 5-6 details a practice script for periods #16 and #17, team, base, par down offense. This script depicts a repetition ratio of five reps for the first offense, four for the seconds, three for the firsts, and finally two for the seconds for a total of 14 repetitions.

Date:				Practice: Tuesday	Periods: 16 & 17	Drill: Team base, par down offense
#	H	D & D	Per	Formation	Play Call	Defense
1	L	1st off	12	Strong Lt Twins	47	Eagle – 4
2	L		21	Zoom Strong Lt Twins	Fake 23 Flood	Over – 2
3	LM		12	Doubles Lt Z Fly	23	Over Bozo Weak – 0
4	M		12	Bear Rt	23 Naked Rt	Over – 4
5	RM		11	Doubles Rt S Fly	20 Trap	Over – 6
6	R	2nd off	12	Shift Unbalanced Lt	47	Over – 3
7	R		21	Weak Rt Twins Zip-Zap	22 Lead	Over M-N Cross – 1
8	R		11	Trey Lt	90 Double In	6-1 Saw – 1
9	R		11	Trips Rt	23 Check 90	Field Blitz – 3
10	RM	1st off	12	Wing Lt Return	25 Force	Field Blitz – 3
11	M		12	Ace Rt	22/23 Check-With-Me	Over – 2
12	LM		21	Zoom Strong Twins Lt	Fake 23 Flood	Eagle – 3
13	L	2nd off	11	Gun Spread Rt	Read Option Rt	Eagle Will Go – 1
14	L		1	Trey Rt	23 Nake Rt Solid	Under – 4

Figure 5-6. An example of a practice script for team, base, par down offense

A variety of coaches could be assigned the responsibility of filling out the practice-period scripts. Some offensive coordinators feel strongly that they, only they, should fill out all of the scripts that are needed for a practice. The underlying premise of this approach is that having the one person most responsible for the actual game play calling be the person who arranges all of the play calling scripts for all of the critical-situation practice scenarios provides the best opportunity to space out the cumulative play call practice needs of the offense. One of the primary downsides of this method is that a tremendous amount of work, and as well of work time, is required of that one individual when this particular method is utilized.

All factors considered, splitting up the practice-period scripting load among the various offensive assistant coaches can be a more efficient means of getting the practice scripts produced. When the assistant coaches become involved in the practice-period scripting, they are a reflection of the "coaching expert" concept.

As a rule, the effort starts out by scripting the two-period (periods #1 and #2), 10-minute, walk-through drill. Having someone script a walk-through drill might come as somewhat of a surprise to some individuals. Truth be known, many coaches firmly believe that the walk-through drill is an extremely important exercise that should be treated with as much focus and attention as any other drill employed during the course of a practice. In each practice, the walk-through drill provides the offensive coordinator with an opportunity to teach, coach, re-teach, and re-coach whatever key offensive concepts that he might feel needs to get emphasized or corrected. Furthermore, with the offensive coordinator in charge of the drill, there should be little doubt about its importance. Accordingly, the offensive coordinator is the coach who usually scripts the walk-through drill.

The offensive line coach takes care of scripting for the unit, inside-run drill that is planned for periods #7 and #8 on Tuesday, as shown in Figure 5-3. Scripting for the unit, inside (9-on-7)-run drill does not include any accompanying passes, a factor that is true, whether the passes are play-action passes or dropback passes.

The unit, 1-on-1 pass drill (periods #11 and #12) is scripted by the wide receiver coach. This exercise is a rapid fire 1-on-1 pass-isolation drill that enables a relatively large number of highly competitive offensive-versus-defensive drill repetitions to be performed. This drill employs a balanced, two-by-two doubles formation. The resultant positioning is to have one receiver (e.g., a tight end, slot back, split end, or flanker) ready to battle a defensive back who is aligned on him in a 1-on-1 pass-completion or pass-defense repetition. Several, usually four or more, quarterbacks rotate from right to left after each competitive repetition. A script is used to tell coaches what pass route the quarterback and receiver will attempt to complete against the covering defender. The unit, 1-on-1 pass drill, which is shown in Figure 5-7, produces a tremendous amount of excitement and competitive energy, as well as a *lot* of pass completion attempts and pass defenses in a relatively short period of time.

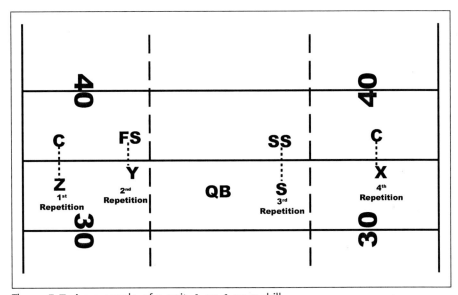

Figure 5-7. An example of a unit, 1-on-1 pass drill

The primary reason that coaches like using this drill so much is because it generates so many quality, competitive, 1-on-1 pass-completion and pass-defense attempts. Furthermore, it is a very easy drill to script. Scripting it basically involves writing out a series of four pass-route attempts (e.g., flanker, tight end, slot, and split end) seven times for a total of 28 repetitions. If the routes begin with the flanker and tight end on the left side of the field on one day, coaches will flip them to the right side the next time this drill is conducted. Pass routes are scripted that the various receivers specifically run. If practice period is ahead of schedule, the entire series is started all over, making sure that the first player to go this time is not the player who went first previously. The objective of this procedure is to ensure that each group of receivers is exposed to a greater degree of route practice variety.

The unit, 7-on-7, skeleton pass drill (periods #13 and #14) is also scripted by the wide receiver coach. To get maximum repetitions, coaches rapid-fire the repetitions of the first and second offense skills-position players one after the other. Since it is Tuesday, the unit, 7-on-7, skeleton pass drill is executed against the scout squad. By going against the scout squad, coaches are able to insert the pass offense that they intend to use against the coverages that they expect to encounter from the next opponent. The rapid-fire repetition action provides an opportunity to get a minimum of eight repetitions each for the first and second offense. As a result, eight pass plays are scripted for the first group, and the same pass plays are then repeated for the second offense. The same plays, however, are not repeated one after the other. Coaches will mix the play call for the second offense as best they can in an attempt to avoid having too many of the same pass play calls performed one after another.

Since it is Tuesday, and third-down offense is one of the game-plan, play call concepts to be practiced this particular day, all of the 7-on-7, skeleton-pass play calls are third-down critical-situation calls, which makes the drill a 7-on-7, third-down skeleton-pass drill. As a result, the first three third-down offense play call repetitions would be from third-and-three to third-and-six. The next three third-down offense play call repetitions would be from third-and-seven to third-and-nine. The last two would be from third-and-ten plus.

It should be noted that as a rule, every week, coaches strive to alter their third-down play delineations slightly. For example, on one particular Tuesday practice, their third-down play breakdowns might be third-and-four, third-and-eight, and third-and-twelve. As discussed previously, coaches generally only script eight plays for the first offense and then repeat those same eight pass plays for the second offense. In addition, they try not to repeat the same two plays in a row with the first and second unit. On the other hand, hash mark calls can, at times, supersede that dictum. A unit, 7-on-7, third-down skeleton-pass script is detailed in Figure 5-8.

Date:			Practice: Tuesday		Periods: 13 & 14	Drill: Third Down 7-on-7 Pass Skelly
#	H	D & D	Per	Formation	Play Call	Defense
1	L	3 + 4	11 (1 off)	Trey Rt	90 double In	Cover 4
2	L	3 + 4	12 (3 off)	Pro Rt	71 F Delay	Cover 4
3	L	3 + 4	11 (1 off)	Zoom Doubles Lt	147 Smash	Cover 2
4	L	3 + 4	11 (2 off)	Trey Rt	90 Double In	Cover 0
5	LM	3 + 4	12 (1 off)	Pro Rt	71 F Delay	Cover 1
6	LM	3 + 4	11 (2 off)	Zoom Doubles Lt	147 Smash	Cover 2
7	M	3 + 8	12 (1 off)	Weak Rt	70 Y Option	Cover 4
8	M	3 + 8	11 (2 off)	Doubles Lt	146 Hank	Cover 3
9	RM	3 + 8	11 (1 off)	Doubles Rt	246 Hank	Cover 1
10	RM	3 + 8	12 (2 off)	Weak Lt	70 Y Option	Cover 6
11	R	3 + 8	11 (1 off)	Trips Rt	Solid 146 Clear	Cover 8
12	R	3 + 8	11 (2 off)	Trips Rt	Solid 146 Clear	Cover 8
13	R	3 + 12	12 (1 off)	Dixie Rt	240 Streaks	Cover 1
14	R	3 + 12	11 (2 off)	Doubles Rt	245 Y X-Dig	Cover 4
15	RM	3 + 12	11 (1 off)	Doubles Rt	245 Y X-Dig	Cover 2
16	RM	3 + 12	12 (2 off)	Dixie Rt	240 Streaks	Cover 3

Figure 5-8. An example of a unit, 7-on-7, third-down skeleton-pass script

Scripting Team Scripts

Although coaches normally try to mix up the structural format of their practices in order to inject variety and a change of pace so that their practices have freshness and avoid staleness, they normally target on focusing on having a full team practice period at the end of practice. That objective doesn't mean that they wouldn't end practice with special teams work or some other facet of game play on occasion. For most coaches, however, the latter periods of practice are the ones toward which coaches usually strive to conduct team practice.

Similar to having the offensive line coach script the unit, inside-run period, the team base, par down offense period is another excellent segment of practice that the offensive line coach can script. This assignment has a lot to do with the fact that the base-run game is an integral aspect in both essential practice focuses. Comparable to the effort to script the unit, inside-run practice periods, coaches start by scripting two practice-play repetitions on the left hash and then move to left-center, the middle of the field, and right-center, before finishing with two practice-play repetitions on the right hash. The second period reverses the order of plays, starting on the right hash and working toward the left hash. As before, the goal is to complete 14 practice repetitions in the allotted two-periods (10 minutes of time).

The aforementioned does not mean that the first and second teams get seven practice-play repetitions in the allotted 10 minutes of practice time. As such, the coaching staff will determine the play-practice repetition ratio. The script of 14 practice-play repetitions might encompass the first five for the first offense, the next four for the second offense, and the final five for the first offense again. This schedule would mean a ten-to-four, first-to-second team play-practice repetition ratio for the two periods. In reality, coaches are responsible for determining what their practice-repetition ratio should be between the first and second offenses.

Practicing with a predetermined run-to-pass ratio is also a factor that needs to be determined by the coaching staff. For example, if the coach's intention is to run in base, par down offensive situations in, approximately, a two-to-one ratio, then their practicing ratio should be in approximately the same quantitative proportion.

The second-and-long situation is an appropriate part of practice that the tight end coach could script. In second-and-long down situations, coaches look to gain first-down yardage from the play being called. At the very worst, they want to make a play call that, when successfully executed, puts the offense in a highly manageable third-and-short to third-and-short-medium situation.

The quarterback coach generally is responsible for scripting third-down yardage situations. Every third-down situation is one that the quarterback coach and his quarterback *must* execute to their best abilities. Third-down offense is a *must* succeed down. Having the quarterback coach handle both the scripting and the coaching of the quarterback's third-down execution is a teaching/coaching combination that can have a critical impact on efforts to successfully convert the ever-so-critical third-down situation.

One scripting situation that most teams leave to the offensive coordinator is blitz control. As has been previously discussed, if coaches are going to go against a defense that is blitz happy, they will often allot extra practice time to work on all of their blitz control techniques, mechanics, and plays. As such, if two periods of blitz control are added to the schedule of team periods, it is the offensive coordinator who will script those extra segments. Furthermore, if coaches are particularly concerned about the blitz abilities of their upcoming opponent, they might use part, or all, of their walk-through period for extra work on blitz-control practice.

All factors considered, two schools of thought exist in the coaching community with regard to how the drill-practice scripts should be placed on the daily practice-plan sheet. One way is to have the drill-practice scripts put on the actual daily practice plan by having the script writer fill out a blank drill-practice script and then give the handwritten copy to a designated person (e.g., a secretary, graduate assistant coach, or manager) to have it typed on the daily-practice plan. Another approach is to have the blank drill-practice script sheet put up on the screen in the offensive staff room, using a computerized scouting program, and then have someone type in the play-by-play information, as the coach responsible for the script calls out each play call. In general, the second method is much more time-efficient and helps to promote an immediate checking of each repetition play call and the subsequent defensive structure to be implemented by the defensive scout squad.

6

Creating the Red Zone Offense Situation Game Plan

Continuing the Big Three of Offensive Play Call Game Planning

Hypothetically, it's now Tuesday evening. The coaches are back from dinner and have just reviewed Tuesday afternoon's practice video. They've checked the practice video to see which portions of their base, par down offense, their second-and-long offense, and their third-down offense meet their expectations. Conversely, they've also looked at which parts of those game-plan, play call concepts they don't feel particularly good about. A few of the latter may be ones that they might consider eliminating. For the remainder of the evening, the coaches try to get a solid start on their last major offensive game planning segment—red zone offense.

Red Zone Significance

The significance of a team being in the red zone is multifaceted. First of all, the vertical distance of the field has shrunk. The maximum vertical distance that the offense has to work in, and that the defense has to defend, is 30 yards when the football is at the very top of the red zone at the plus 20-yard line. Those 30 red zone yards encompass the 20 vertical yards to the goal line and the 10 vertical yards of the end zone. In addition, as the offense closes in on the goal line, that vertical distance that the offense has to work in decreases with every yard the offense gets closer to the goal line. As a result, as the offense closes in on the goal line, it has fewer and fewer vertical yards in which their upfield, vertical pass routes can work. As a result, such routes have to be adjusted within the shrunken vertical distance. The other key consideration is that pass patterns have to be called in which the routes utilized *will* have enough vertical distance to work in.

In the opposite vein, the offense has to also be aware of the fact that the defense gains the advantage of having to defend less and less vertical distance as the football closes in on the goal line. Undoubtedly, both the offense and the defense would both agree that the closer the offense gets to the goal line, the greater its chances of scoring either a touchdown or a field goal. On the other hand, the fact remains that as the football gets closer and closer to the goal line, the defense has the ever-growing advantage of having less and less vertical distance to have to pass defend.

Another key significance of the red zone is the factor that the defense *is* backed up and is on its heels. If the offense has been driving, then whatever the defense has been doing has not been working. Whether that scenario is the situation or not, many red zone defenses, at that point, will increase their level of frontal-stunt and secondary-blitz pressure in an attempt to shake things up and make things happen for themselves.

Red Zone Delineations

For me personally, red zone offense is offense on, or inside, the plus 20-yard line, attempting to score. It should be noted that some coaches designate the 30-yard line or the 25-yard line as the start of the red zone. Most coaches, however, subscribe to the more traditional belief of the 20-yard line as the start of the red zone. Most coaches have delineation breakdowns within the red zone and outside of the actual red zone that are very important to them.

For example, some coaches actually start their red zone contemplations with what is referred to as the "deep red zone." To them, the deep red zone is the area from the plus 40-yard line to the top of the actual red zone on the 20-yard line. One of the factors that many coaches are concerned with as soon as they get to the red zone is the fact that their vertical-pass attack encounters the problem of having a diminished vertical throwing distance in which to work. As a rule, throwing from the deep red zone allows teams almost all of the pass weaponry that they would have from anywhere else on the field.

The next red zone delineation to be considered is what is often termed as the "black zone." The black zone is any area inside the plus 10-yard line, in which it is no longer possible for an offense to earn a first down. In reality, this area can be anywhere from the plus 10-yard line to wherever goal line offense may start. The black zone often needs special pass pattern and route considerations because of the extreme lack of vertical field distance in which to operate. The offense may also be limited when the defense employs a special pass coverage in this area, such as seven-across zone coverage, which can make it extremely difficult to throw the football.

The final breakdown delineation of the red zone is the "goal line zone." How teams view what constitutes goal line play can vary from team to team and game to game. Much of this characterization will depend on the style of play of the offense and/or the defense. Most teams will consider the offense as goal line offense when the offense uses extra big personnel, such as extra tight ends, "H" backs, or fullbacks. A defense can be considered as employing its goal line defense when it puts extra defensive linemen, linebackers, or safeties into the game. As a rule, more often than not, such defensive goal line substitutions are undertaken in an effort to match up their big personnel with the big, goal line personnel that the offense has sent in. Furthermore, as part of their goal line efforts, most coaches culminate their red zone thinking with their two-point play offense.

Creating a Deep Red Zone Game Plan

As a rule, coaches can look to their deep red zone play call list any time they cross the plus 40-yard line going in. On the other hand, coaches also like to call a play from their deep red zone play call list after just executing a big play, or two, with their run or pass game. Since the defense tends to be reeling from such big, quick gains, it can be a particularly suitable opportunity to take a deep-pass play shot to the end zone. This shot could be anything coaches feel might succeed, including something as simple as one of their normal, deep dropback or play-action passes.

The deep red zone is also an area where teams like to consider using a trick play, especially a deep, trick-type pass play. Getting to the deep red zone does not automatically mean that coaches are going to call for a deep pass or utilize a deep special- or trick-type of pass play. Quite the contrary, coaches might, conversely, choose to stay within the guidelines of their base offensive attack and employ their run or pass ball-control attack to eat up the clock and score. If they are coming off a successful, big-play gain, coaches tend to be very careful, if they use pass plays, to make sure that they have good blitz beaters built into them. This measure is essential in case the defense wants to take a chance and go after the offense with some sort of frontal pressure and/or blitz.

Most coaches do not have a large deep red zone game-plan, play call list. In this area, the basic objective is to have a relatively small, fixed amount of deep-pass or deep trick-pass plays that can be effectively utilized in this area of the field. This step is undertaken before coaches start to get into the red zone, with its more limited north-south vertical yardage distances in which their pass game can work.

In order to develop their deep red zone game-plan, play call list, coaches perform a very specific analysis of video breakdowns of plays that have created opportunities in the deep red zone. That analysis includes determining certain factors. For example, what does their opponent do in these situations? Do they sit back and play base defense? Do they go on the attack and bring frontal-stunt and/or blitz pressure? Based on their dissection of that information, they then attempt to identify possible big-play calls that could produce quick-strike, big-play yardage and/or scores. Figure 6-1 illustrates an example of a purposely small, deep red zone game-plan, play call list.

DEEP RED ZONE

<u>PASS</u>

DOUBLES LT 246 DOUBLE POST   DOUBLES RT 146 DOUBLE POST
TREY RT FLEX 140 Y READ   TREY LT FLEX 240 Y READ
DOUBLES RT S REVERSE DOUBLE PASS QB

Figure 6-1. An example of a deep red zone game-plan, play call list

Creating a Red Zone Run Play Call Game Plan

Hypothetically, your team has just gotten to, or into, the red zone. The defense is reeling from a drive that has already encompassed, potentially, up to 60 yards. You, however, are not taking the situation for granted. Your experience tells you that all of the efforts involved in the excellent drive to this point may be for naught if you fail in the red zone.

As has been previously noted, red zone offense is one of three, key game-plan elements, along with base, par down offense and third-down offense. Red zone offense is another statistical area that most coaches analyze carefully each week to determine the extent to which it is working and whether adjustments need to be made. In reality, some teams are able to move the ball up and down the field and rank high statistically in total offense, but continually sputter in the red zone.

The bottom-line issue with regard to red zone offense is whether a team can get the football into the end zone once it's in the red zone or does it have to settle for a field goal. Obviously, a much worse scenario would be to come away from its red zone effort with no points at all. Failure in the red zone can be devastating, which is why red zone offense is one of the three, key game-plan phases and why coaches put so much effort into their red zone offense game and practice planning.

Coaches start their red zone offense game-plan, play call efforts with the run game. Since statistics indicate that they will only be in the red zone a limited amount of times per game, coaches strive to have a *very* tight run-*and*-pass-game plan. When they initially undertake their red zone offense run-game planning, they immediately look to their base, par down offense run-game plan. As such, they focus on what they believe, to this point, are their *very best* play calls from that list. They then carefully study and analyze their opponent's red zone defense to confirm which are their best runs to utilize in combination with their personnel plans, formations, shifts, and motions.

A key point, in this regard, is that by employing your very best run-game concepts, your players will be executing what they know best. The red zone is not a time for new run plays or strange formations, shifts, or motions. Instead, all coaches want their red zone offense plan to be executed with confidence, grit, and determination by their players. The athletes are the ones who have to put the football in the end zone, and coaches don't want to hold them back by confronting them with uncertainty and doubt.

One underlying principle of an effective red zone offense that coaches should adopt is to utilize runs and formations that are effective against frontal stunts and secondary blitzes. A key focus for many red zone defenses is to try to put the brakes on the offense's advances with blitz pressure. To counter that tactic, coaches should consider avoiding, or at least limiting, the use of short-edge (i.e., no tight end) formations against a blitzing defense that frequently employs outside pressures. Instead, coaches could use two- and three-tight end formations and formations with wing alignments that can help widen such outside pressures, which makes them less effective.

The aforementioned doesn't mean that coaches shouldn't use spread formations or any type of specific personnel plan, formation, shift, or motion. Rather, it means that, from carefully studying red zone video, coaches need to determine the most effective run plays, with accompanying personnel plans, formations, shifts, and motions that can help teams to be successful against the red zone defenses that they are expecting to see from their opponent.

Coaches are looking for run efficiency. They do not want negative-yardage plays. They want an attacking, north-south run game that, at the least, will put them in manageable, third-down yardage situations.

For some teams, their inside- and outside-run zone plays can provide them with the effective, straight ahead, north-south run plays that they need. For other teams, it might be their dive/counter series or their sweep/belly action. Quick, inside trap action and draws can also be very effective against a pressuring red zone defense. This scenario can be especially true if trap and draw games are not a big part of their offense in other game situations. In that situation, they can employ their trap and draw games to surprise a pressuring, blitzing red zone defense that is not expecting such run action.

If coaches have an option offense, whether from under the center or from a spread, shotgun set, they can also effectively attack red zone defenses. For example, run options can do a lot to discourage a pressuring, blitz red zone defense. Quite simply, it's hard to frontal stunt and/or secondary blitz when the defense knows it has to be assignment-oriented with regard to who is assigned to the dive/running back, who has the quarterback, and who has the pitch back. This factor applies, whether the option-action is double or triple option.

Reverses and counters have also been shown to be very effective in the red zone. Given that red zone defenses tend to be so intensely locked into stopping the base run and pass attack of their opponent, they often become extremely vulnerable to reverses and counters. In reality, the same point can be made for trick plays by the offense in the red zone. Whether it is a special, trick run or pass play, the profound demands involved with stopping the offense in the red zone seem to make the usage of such special, trick plays particularly effective.

Creating a Red Zone Pass Play Call Game Plan

With regard to creating a red zone pass play call game plan, two major red zone offense concerns need to be considered. Both factors have been previously discussed. The first point is the fact that a red zone passing attack has to deal with the diminished vertical distance of the red zone. If the football is on the 20-yard line, teams only have 30 vertical yards total in which its red zone offense can work. Furthermore, as the red zone offense progresses toward the end zone, the vertical distance of the red zone shrinks accordingly. As a result, deep pass patterns and routes may have to be adjusted to the contour of a shrunken red zone area. For example, what does a receiver performing a streak route do when he runs out of room and approaches the corner of the end zone's back line? The chances are that the receiver executing a streak route will have to break flat to the inside, a yard from the back line.

Likewise, a post-corner route should stem only six or seven yards into the end zone and then round out the corner-break portion of the route to use as much of the end zone's back end-line area as possible. Such an action would permit a post-corner route to maintain a maximum amount of distance from, for example, a flat route that works just over the goal line. An overview of the modification needs of deep routes in the red zone area is detailed in Figure 6-2.

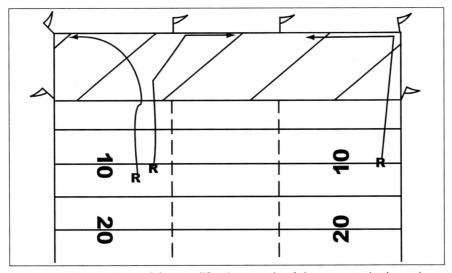

Figure 6-2. An overview of the modification needs of deep routes in the red zone

If red zone offense patterns and routes don't make the essential adjustments that are required because of the limited amount of vertical yardage that the red zone has, then at lease some of those pass patterns and route combinations can run together, relative to both their vertical and lateral separations. Cluttered pass patterns and route combinations may result in a situation where a single pass defender may very well be able to cover two, if not more, pass receivers. More often than not, such cluttered pass patterns and route combinations are a major cause of interceptions.

Figure 6-3 shows a cluttered route pass pattern. For example, the streak route, stuck in the corner of the end zone, forces a cluttering of the streak and post-corner route. In turn, the failure of the flat route to stretch his lateral course just one yard over the goal line (a basic rule for flat routes in the end-zone area) can create even more route cluttering. This situation does not mean that flood pattern action (the pass-pattern action illustrated in Figure 6-3) should not be utilized. Rather, it refers to the fact that pass patterns, such as floods, have to be very concerned with having a proper amount of room in which to operate. If an adequate amount of room to operate in doesn't exist, adjustments must be made in the pass pattern and/or route that enable those patterns and routes to work in tightened areas of the red zone, black zone, or goal line.

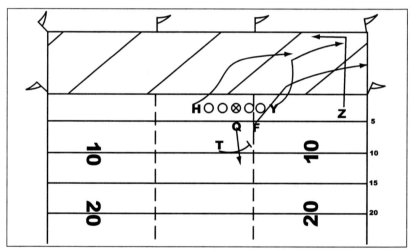

Figure 6-3. An example of a cluttered pass pattern in the end zone

The second factor that should be considered when developing a red zone pass play call game plan is the need for anti-blitz pass thinking. Many defensive coaches view red zone defense as involving a situation in which the defense has its back to the wall and needs to undertake specific measures that will help put the brakes on the offense in order to prevent it from scoring. In this scenario, the defense needs either a turnover or a "stop" and may do whatever it can to make one happen. Nor surprisingly, both the red zone offense *and* red zone defense are thinking blitz … red zone frontal-stunt and blitz pressure by the defense and red zone anti-blitz control by the offense.

As the football gets closer and closer to the goal line, the defensive secondary comes to realize that it has to cover less and less territory, which can be considered an advantage for it. On the other hand, it also has to realize that a short, quick throw from the quarterback can be devastating. At a minimum, it can result in a completion that gains a significant red zone yardage.

Most coaches firmly believe that anti-blitz passing starts with quick-pass game thinking and quickly thrown play-action passing. In reality, many coaches employ such an anti-blitz pass mentality for their play call game planning almost anywhere on the field. It has very particular importance, however, when the offense is in the red zone because of the defense's efforts to put pressure on the offense with frontal-stunt pressure and/or secondary blitzes.

Coaches study breakdown video of their opponent's red zone defense to try to determine which of their quick, pass-game patterns and routes can be successful against the opposition's defensive efforts. In addition, they analyze their opponent to decide which personnel plans, formations, shifts, or motions can provide them with their best chance for success by creating formational or personnel mismatches. They then follow that course of planning to see which of their quickly executed play-action passes can be as effective as their quick-pass, red zone play call game plan.

The quick-pass game, whether by three-step drop or play-action, can help a team's red zone offense against defensive-blitz pressure by getting the football thrown quickly. In addition, a quick-pass game completion in the red zone typically means sizeable yardage. It should be remembered that in the red zone, teams only have a maximum of 20 yards to go to score six points, and frequently, the shrunken red zone distance entails far less yardage to cross the goal line.

Five-step dropback pass action can also be very effective in the red zone. The primary concern about employing such five-step drop action in the red zone is that both the pass pattern and the pass-route action must be quick to address the pass-protection needs of the offense that may arise due to possible heavy frontal-stunt action and/or secondary-blitz pressure. As stated previously, deep routes that may be a part of such pass patterns must be able to make any adjustments that are needed as a result of the vertically shortened red zone area.

Seven-step dropback action in the red zone is an occurrence that, for the most part, that should be avoided. Seven-step drop, timed patterns take a lot of time to unfold, which involves a lot of protection time, often in the midst of heavy defensive-blitz pressure. In addition, seven-step drop patterns frequently entail deep-yardage throwing and routes, which the vertically shortened red zone may not allow enough room in which to operate. The same factor is true for more delayed timed play-action passes, designed to be executed off of seven-step drop action.

The five-step drop, timed pass patterns and route combinations that are red zone-friendly are initially short, quick-isolation routes. On the other hand, the actual pass patterns, routes, and route combinations utilized will have as much to do with the pass coverages employed by the opponent's red zone defense as anything. Initially, most red zone defenses focus on whether to blitz and how to best employ man coverage to support their efforts to blitz. Of course, a red zone defense could utilize a zone-blitz defense, which would present its own set of problems. In reality, however short, quick-isolation routes, such as wide receiver comeback-out routes, and isolation-option routes, such as slot options, running-back options, and tight end options, are relatively simple routes that can be very effective in the red zone against either man or zone coverages.

Crossing routes can also be especially effective as five-step drop, timed pass patterns in the red zone against both man or zone coverages. A key factor, as stated previously, is to make sure that all pass patterns in the red zone offense feature a quickly executed design in order to help counter defensive blitzing. The crossing-route pass patterns can be inside crossing patterns, such as the one detailed in Figure 6-4 or an outside-type, crossing-route combination, as shown in Figure 6-5.

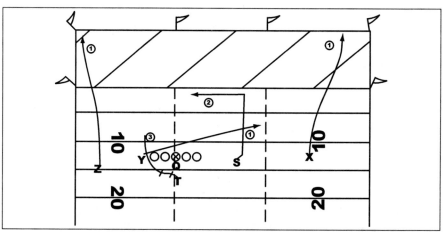

Figure 6-4. An example of an inside crossing route combination in the red zone

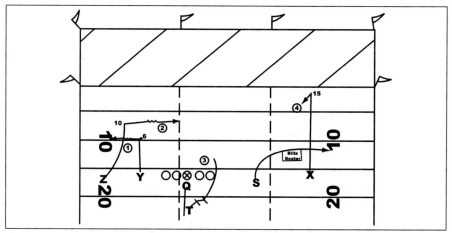

Figure 6-5. An example of an outside crossing route combination in the red zone

Drive-route pattern principles have also been found to be very effective when incorporated in a red zone pass attack. An example of a pass play that utilizes a drive-route pattern principle is shown in Figure 6-6.

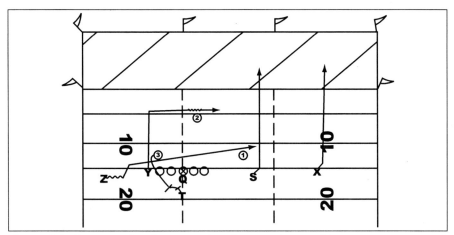

Figure 6-6. An example of a pass play that employs a drive-route pass pattern principle in the red zone

All of the aforementioned five-step drop, timed pass patterns are quickly timed pattern concepts that have built-in blitz-beater routes to help control the possibility of defensive blitzing in the red zone. When sight-adjusting concepts and hot-and-warm blitz-beater routes are incorporated into the pass attack, additional blitz controls are then available to make such five-step drop, timed pass patterns more effective against red zone defenses.

Isolations routes, crossing routes, and drive routes are a few of the five-step drop, timed pass patterns that can be successfully employed in the red zone. Pass patterns that are built around streaks, post, and post-corner routes are other possible five-step drop, timed pass routes that have been shown to be very effective in the red zone. On the other hand, as has been stated previously, the problem of having sufficient vertical distance in the red zone to execute such pass routes is a definite concern.

Furthermore, executing such deeper and more delayed, timed pass routes can also be greatly impeded by the delayed timing involved in trying to execute such deeper pass routes that take longer to unfold. Quite simply, longer, more delayed, timed-pass actions require pass protection that has to be held longer. This factor can be quite a difficult chore against blitzing, red zone defenses. In reality, as needed route depth and pass execution timing can be shortened and adjusted to fit the situational parameters of red zone passing. Figure 6-7 illustrates how a normally deep, seven-step route stem, post-corner route can be altered for use in the red zone by shortening the stem of the post-corner routes to five steps. Such a red zone alteration allows for quicker pass-action execution by the quarterback, which, in turn, necessitates less protection time.

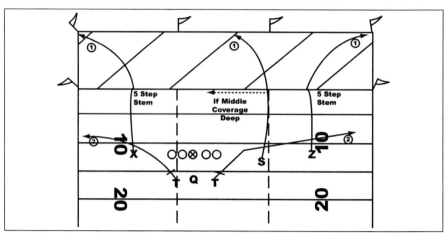

Figure 6-7. An example of adjusting a seven-step, timed, post-corner pass pattern to five-step timing for red zone usage

All of the aforementioned steps and measures can help the offense be better able to control and exploit any blitz-pressure threats by the red zone defense.

Sprint-out passing can also be very effective in the red zone. Similar to the underlying design of run-option action, sprint-out action puts an extra factor into play in attacking red zone defenses. In run-option action, it is the additional threat of the quarterback keeping the football and being a legitimate run threat that can put so much pressure on the defense. Sprint-out passing can involve a comparable dimension, given that the quarterback can either run the football or pass it as a run-pass option. If the defense rolls up to take away the ability of the quarterback to run, it is quite likely that a pass receiver will be left open in front of him to receive a pass. If the defense stays off the quarterback and drops back into full pass coverage, a running quarterback will be presented with a better-than-average opportunity to run for a sizeable gain. It should be noted that a sizeable gain in the red zone will put the red zone offense that much closer to the goal line.

In addition, bootleg, naked bootleg, and waggle play-action pass action can be very productive in the red zone, given that the misdirection action of these pass plays can place substantial stress on a red zone defense that is pursuing hard to the threat of a run. Furthermore, much like sprint-out pass-action, the bootleg or waggle quarterback can help put the threat of quarterback run/pass action into play.

Screens carry a very big part of the pass-game plan of many coaches in their red zone offense. For example, screens can be a very viable means of attacking red zone defenses that blitz. Being aware of and understanding the wide variety of defensive blitzes that can be utilized in the red zone can help the offense plan and determine which type of screens are best suited to counter particular defensive efforts in the red zone. With regard to screens, offenses have a number of possible alternatives from which to choose, including slow-developing screens, quick screens, outside screens, off-tackle screens, and middle screens. In order to ensure that their screen game is sound, coaches need to carefully evaluate their choices, based on the red zone tendencies of their defensive opponent. The primary goal of the offense, in this regard, is to make the screen game an effective part of its red zone offense game play call list.

Figure 6-8 illustrates an example of a red zone play call game plan. As a rule, most coaches try to finish their red zone play call game plan by the time they leave the office Tuesday evening. As a result, they are prepared to address the remainder of their red zone play call game planning, including the black zone, goal line, and two-point play call game plans on Wednesday morning.

RED ZONE

RUNS

DIXIE LT 22 CHECK 90	DIXIE RT 23 CHECK 90
ACE RT 24/25 CHECK-WITH-ME	ACE LT 24/25 CHECK-WITH-ME
ACE RT OVER 22/23 CHECK-WITH-ME	ACE LT OVER 22/23 CHECK-WITH-ME
HO WING LT 47	HO WING RT 46
STEM UNBALANCED STRONG RT 22 LEAD	STEM UNBALANCED STRONG LT 23 LEAD
STRONG PRO LT 23 LEAD Z REVERSE	STRONG PRO RT 22 LEAD Z REVERSE
GUN SPREAD RT READ OPTION RT	GUN SPREAD LT READ OPTION LT
TREY RT SOCKET 20 TRAP	TREY LT SOCKET 21 TRAP
SHIFT WING RT 24 FORCE	SHIFT WING LT 25 FORCE

PASS

DIXIE LT 93 INSIDE	DIXIE RT 93 INSIDE
SHIFT DOUBLES LT 92 DOUBLE SLANT	SHIFT DOUBLES RT 92 DOUBLES SLANT
WEAK RT ACROSS 79 Y DELAY	WEAK LT ACROSS 79 Y DELAY
SHIFT WEAK LT TWINS FAKE 22 SMASH	SHIFT WEAK RT TWINS FAKE 23 SMASH
DOUBLES LT 145 Y/S CROSS	DOUBLES RT 245 Y/S CROSS
DIXIE LT 147 SMASH	DIXIE RT 247 SMASH
SHIFT TREY RT 93 DOUBLE OUT	SHIFT TREY LT 93 DOUBLE OUT

Figure 6-8. An example of a red zone game-plan, play call list

The Black Zone

As stated previously, the black zone is any area inside the plus 10-yard line—a space in which the offense can no longer gain a first down. Accordingly, this area can be anywhere from the plus 10-yard line to whatever point at which the goal line offense or defense may start. This area of the red zone is categorized as the black zone for a number of very distinct reasons. First of all, the offense is definitely running out of room with regard to the vertical amount of distance in which it has to work. Second, many red zone defenses, because they are aware of the fact that they have a very limited amount of vertical area that they have to pass defend, can often use different types of pass coverages in the black zone. Third, the possible shift to more basic zone pass coverages in the black zone by the defense can further translate to the defense having a more basic, non-blitzing attitude.

If the football is on the 10-yard line, the black zone offense has a maximum vertical distance of 20 yards in which to work. In turn, if the football is on the four-yard line, the offense has only 14 yards of vertical distance in which to work. As a result, the offense has to employ pass routes and patterns that can be effective in such a shortened vertical area. This factor often necessitates employing very specific and specially designed pass patterns that may not be used anywhere else on the field. Because the defense in the black zone is also quite aware of the shrunken vertical distance it has to defend, it can utilize various forms of a seven (pass defenders) –across, zone coverage, as detailed in Figure 6-9. All factors considered, such a coverage can easily negate the effectiveness of many of the offense's base pass patterns, as well as many of its more specific red zone pass patterns.

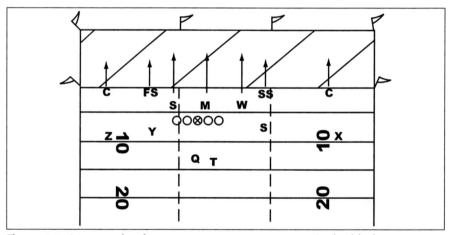

Figure 6-9. An example of a seven-across zone coverage in the black zone

Creating a Black Zone Play Call Game Plan

The play call game plan for the black zone offense is heavily based on the need for very specific pass patterns and route combinations that can work within a very limited amount of vertical-yardage distance. Furthermore, as discussed previously, such pass patterns may have to work against coverages that can be different from any opponent coverages used elsewhere on the field or in other game-type situations. These circumstances do not mean that an analysis or consideration for the run game does not occur in the black zone. As a rule, however, most coaches normally apply their red zone run-game reasoning into the black zone as well, although, on occasion, a run-play thought or two for the black zone may vary from the run-game plan that has been devised for the red zone offense. When that situation occurs, coaches simply list such run-play calls into the section of their red zone play call sheet that is designated for their black zone offense play call game plan.

As such, the primary focus of the black zone play call game plan is the pass game. Some of the passes that coaches include in their red zone offense, pass-game plan will fit very well into their pass play call game plan for the black zone offense. This factor is often particularly true with many of their quick, three-step drop pass patterns and their quick, play-action passes. Pass patterns that are specifically designed for the black zone tend to focus on either isolation routes, such as fade routes, fade comeback-out routes, option routes, and/or quick, double move-type routes, such as tight end stick-and-go routes. Examples of black zone routes are detailed in Figure 6-10.

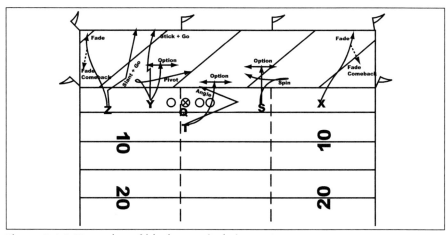

Figure 6-10. Examples of black zone isolation routes

For many teams, a major part of their black zone pass attack focuses on routes, route combinations, and patterns that produce high/low read route combinations, and flood-route patterns. These pass concepts try to utilize every vertical and horizontal piece of territory that is a part of the end zone, which allows for the greatest horizontal and lateral displacement of the receivers in the end zone as possible. Figure 6-11 provides an example of a high/low route combination pattern—a tight end and a slot working low routes and outside wide receivers performing short post routes high in an effort to isolate seven-across coverage defenders with high-low reads. Figure 6-12 shows a naked bootleg flood black zone pass pattern, which depicts an effort to flood the end zone with a maximum usage of the end zone area through targeted route displacement. Figure 6-13 outlines an example of a black zone game-plan, play call list.

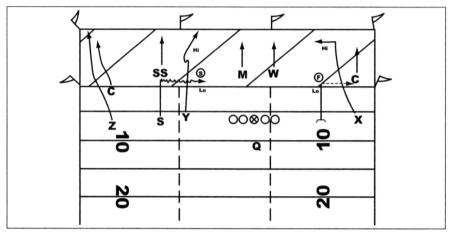

Figure 6-11. An example of a high/low black zone pass pattern, isolating seven-across black zone coverage (isolating "S" linebacker and "F" safety)

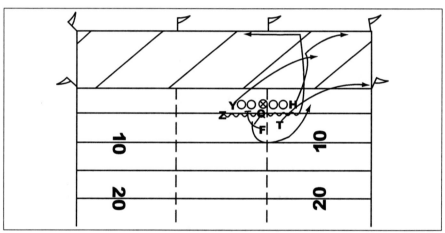

Figure 6-12. An example of a naked bootleg flood black zone pass pattern, with maximum route displacement of the end zone

---

BLACK ZONE

PASS

DOUBLES LT FLEX 140 RAPTOR	DOUBLES RT FLEX 240 RAPTOR
TRIPS LT 140 Y NOD DOUBLE IN	TRIPS RT 240 Y NOD DOUBLE IN
SHIFT STRONG WING RT 78 F ANGLE	SHIFT STRONG WING LT 78 F ANGLE
SHIFT DOUBLES LT 93	SHIFT DOUBLES RT 93
TREY RT 92 SLANT	TREY LT 92 SLANT

Figure 6-13. An example of a black zone game-plan, play call list

The Goal Line

The final phase of the red zone planning that needs to be addressed is the goal line zone. In reality, the delineation of goal line play can vary from team to team and game to game, depending on the style of play of the offense and/or the defense. Most teams treat their offensive attack as a goal line offense when their offense employs extra big personnel, such as tight ends, "H" backs, or fullbacks. In a similar vein, as stated previously, defenses are thought to be utilizing their goal line defense when they put extra defensive linemen, linebackers, or safeties into the game. More often than not, such defensive goal line substitutions are made in an effort to match up big personnel when the offense sends in its big, goal line personnel.

As a rule, most goal line offenses and defense start somewhere around the three- to four-yard line. It should be noted that even if offenses are on their opponent's one- or two-yard line does not mean that they have to insert extra, big personnel into the game. One question that often arises is whether a goal line offense can use their normal personnel (i.e., two running backs, one tight end, and two wide receivers) or their two-tight-end personnel (i.e., one running back, two tight ends, and two wide receivers) to execute their goal line offense. Of course they can, and many often do. In fact, some teams continue using their spread personnel (i.e., one running back, no tight end, and four wide receivers) formation offensive thinking all the way down to the actual goal line.

Besides the issue of either side of the ball employing "big" personnel, the other key concern for goal line offenses is the fact that goal line defenses tend to take on special structural designs of their own near the goal line. For the most part, goal line defenses are designed to load up to stop the run. Given the limited vertical distance that they have to pass defend, most goal line defenses move their safeties up to, in essence, act as extra run-stoppage linebackers. Certain defensive fronts that are utilized on the goal line, for example, 6-2 and 6-5 fronts, double eagle "Bear" fronts, and 5-3 stack fronts, all present radically different defensive fronts from what is normally seen most anywhere else on the field. As a result, blocking schemes have to be retargeted and adjusted to make sure that every defender at the point of attack is blocked.

Creating a Goal Line Run Play Call Game Plan

When the offense gets the football down close to the goal line, the run game certainly gets more and more inviting. For example, first-and-goal on the three-yard line means that a team has three and perhaps four shots to run the football into the end zone. As such, it only needs to average one yard, or less, per carry to score. In other words, one soundly executed run for a three- or four-yard game will, most likely, result in six points. When that thinking is tied into the fact that goal line offense passing has an extremely limited amount of vertical passing distance to work, which makes successful goal line passing all-the-more difficult and a hard-nosed, downhill run game look all-the-more inviting.

Truth be known, however, running the football on goal line situations can be a lot easier said than actually done. On the other hand, it can be *very* hard for a defense to take a sound run game on head to head, when such short-yardage amounts are needed. The bottom line is that unless a goal line offense or defense has an overwhelming talent or power advantage, running the ball and defensing the run on the goal line normally lead to "war" on the line of scrimmage.

In reality, creating a play call game plan for goal line situations is no different than creating a play call game plan for any other critical game-plan situation. As in other phases of offensive game planning, coaches carefully study video breakdowns of their opponent's defensive efforts on the goal line in previous games. Such study addresses a number of issues. For example, what type of goal line defense, or defenses, does their opponent employ? What type of coverages? Does the goal line defense use frontal stunts and/or blitzes? Collectively, the answers to such questions help to determine what the goal line offense needs to do to combat the defense's efforts on the goal line.

No matter what type of running-game attack a team might utilize, employing two-tight end formations can greatly help to stretch goal line defenses laterally. In addition, the use of wing back-type blockers can further help to stretch, or thin, a goal line defensive front. Another benefit of utilizing either such wing-back blockers or widely aligned fullback-types can help block outside, defensive edge, rush-type defenders. Figure 6-14 provides an example of a two-tight-end, goal line offensive formation that includes both a wing back and a widely aligned fullback.

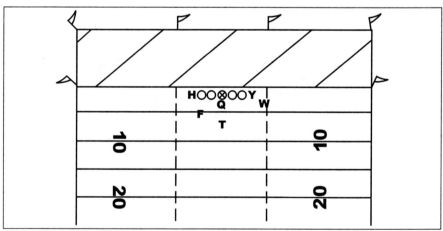

Figure 6-14. An example of a two-tight-end, goal line formation, with a wing back and a widely aligned fullback

Another key goal line offense issue that coaches need to address is whether to insert "big" personnel into the game to combat any extra "big" personnel substitutes of a goal line defense. More often than not, goal line defenses often employ extra defensive tackles, defensive ends, linebackers, or safeties to beef up their fronts in the goal zone area in an effort to stop the offense's run-play efforts, which is a major reason that many goal line offenses utilize extra tight ends and fullback-types in their personnel plan approaches on the goal line.

Another issue that coaches have to give attention to in the goal line area is what type of run plays they should use in their run attack in that part of the field. Much of the answer to that factor should be based on their overall offensive run-game philosophy. In fact, the first place for coaches to start in planning their goal line run package is to determine what, in their base run-game package, can be effective as part of their goal line run package. For example, does their base, run package contain an off-tackle power, a straight ahead isolation/blast, or a sweep toss play? As a rule, such run plays can be excellent goal line run plays. Another key point to keep in mind is that the fact that one of the best things about the usage of such run plays as part of their goal line run package is that they are run plays that their offensive players know and have practiced over and over.

Run-option plays can also be excellent run plays that can be incorporated as part of a team's goal line offense run package. As such, aggressive, attacking goal line defenses can be slowed down significantly with run-option plays, given the fact that defenses suddenly have to become run-option assignment-oriented, rather than gap-control oriented.

The aforementioned doesn't mean that teams shouldn't use run plays on goal line situations that are not a part of their base, run game package. In fact, running a straight-ahead, lead-block, isolation blast play as part of a goal line run package is a sound goal line concept, just as long as it is already a constant part of that team's goal line offense package. The other good thing about having an isolation run play as a part of a team's goal line run package is that it the type of play that can be very effective as a part of its third-and-short run-game package.

An instance in which some coaches get in trouble is when they try to install a run play that they saw being run very effectively on video against their next opponent by another team—a play that is rather foreign to the type of run plays that would normally be a part of the goal line offensive package for those coaches. For example, while the off-tackle power play can be an excellent run play on the goal line, it is a high-maintenance play, with regard to its teaching, coaching, and player execution. Such a play is not the type of play that most coaches would like to newly install in practice on a Tuesday or Wednesday, given how important its usage would be on a critical-situation goal line play. The other factor to keep in mind with regard to installing new goal line run plays is the fact that the defense's goal line, front structure may be radically different from what may be seen by the offense during the rest of the game. For example, learning a new run play, with all its blocking intricacies against a 6-2, 6-5, double eagle "Bear," or a 5-3 stack goal line defense, may be more than can be adequately handled in such a critical-situation area as the goal line.

Another point that should be considered with regard to the run-game attack in goal line offense is to utilize outside or off-tackle run plays that involve blocking normally, more hard-hitting, physically strong safety- and linebacker-types and leaving cornerbacks unblocked. When a blocking design cannot account for the block of every defender at the point of attack, leaving the cornerback alone as the unblocked defender can be a very effective tactic. The underlying premise of such a strategy is to block the bigger, more-physical goal line defenders and force the often smaller and less-physical cornerbacks to take on the running back one-on-one. Quite often, such a tactic can force such a cornerback to try and make a tackle for no or a very limited amount of yardage. If the running back is a physical runner, this assignment can be very tough for the cornerback to successfully execute.

Creating a Goal Line Pass Play Call Game Plan

In reality, much of a goal line offense's pass attack has already been discussed and determined, since many of the goal line pass patterns that are to be utilized can come directly from a team's black zone pass play call game-plan list. The goal line area places many of the same limitations on the offense's passing attack as the black zone does, particularly with regard to having an extremely limited amount of vertical passing distance in which to work. In reality, the only real difference between passing in the black zone and passing in the goal line area is about one to three vertical-distance yards in which the goal line offense can work. As a result, the primary focus of most coaches for their goal line, pass play game plan is to either utilize one of the black zone passes that they feel can work well in the goal line area or any of their play-action passes that complement their more formal, heavy-personnel goal line formations and run plays.

The two most commonly employed play-action passes in the goal line offense of many teams are quick, play-action pass flood patterns and naked bootleg passes. Coaches tend to like both of these kinds of passes, because both of these passing concepts are often employed throughout the execution of their offense, anywhere on the field. As a result, coaches are amenable to using play-action pass concepts on the goal line, given the fact that they have been practiced over and over, as contingency possibilities for a large number of critical-situation play-downs throughout a game. In other words, their offense should be very familiar with both passing concepts, given their constant practice repetitions. It should be noted that on occasion, teams will change up their formational looks to help disguise both of these play-action, pass play concepts. The use of shifts and motions can also be employed in order to give the defense a variety of looks (including some that are unfamiliar) to contend with on the goal line.

The aforementioned certainly doesn't mean that these are the only types of pass plays that teams will utilize on the goal line. In fact, most teams have other goal line pass plays in their arsenal. For example, Figure 6-15 details one such play—a crossing

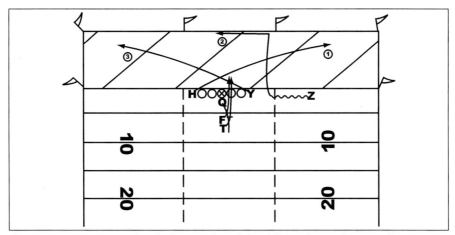

Figure 6-15. An example of a longer timed, goal line, play-action crossing pattern

pattern off of more delayed isolation/blast faking action. Many teams like to execute this particular play-action play from the one- or two-yard line. Although a question would arise about why teams would consider using a more delayed, timed play-action pass from inside the two-yard line that normally would require a longer amount of protection timing, the underlying premise of such a decision is sound. As such, inside the two-yard line, an over-the-top, jumping isolation/blast play will likely cause the outside defenders to close down hard on a good fake by the quarterback and tailback in an effort to tackle the tailback. Such hard, down-the-line pursuit angles by the outside rushers, in response to the fake, should help the quarterback to have sufficient time to set up to read the meshing, crossing action of the split end and the tight end and the delayed over-the-middle inside square-in route of the flanker. Had the line of scrimmage been on the four- or five-yard line, the end-of-line defensive rushers might have been on a rush course that would allow them to attack the fake mesh point and still be able to easily redirect to the quarterback, once they realized that the tailback was only faking.

On occasion, trick plays have also been found to be very effective in offensive situations on the goal line. Since the goal line defense is often tightly wound up in its efforts to strike quickly to the flow of the football in order to make an all-important stop, goal line defenses can be very susceptible to trick (i.e., special) plays. For example, counter actions can be employed to successfully attack the fast pursuit flows of the defensive front. As such, naked bootleg and waggle action, in the pass game, can produce excellent counter-action. Since run counter-action can easily be disturbed by defensive penetration, run counter-action should be utilized only if a goal line offense is well-drilled and practiced in counter run blocking cut-off and seal-blocking skills.

Reverses can also do an exceptional job of creating counter-action, as well as serve as trick (i.e., special) plays, if the situation merits. As discussed previously, employing the element of surprise against a pressure-happy, goal line defense can enable trick plays to be a very viable way to attacking a goal line defense. Figure 6-16 provides an example of a tailback pass in the goal line area against a 6-2 goal line defense. Figure 6-17 details a game-plan, play call list for a goal line offense.

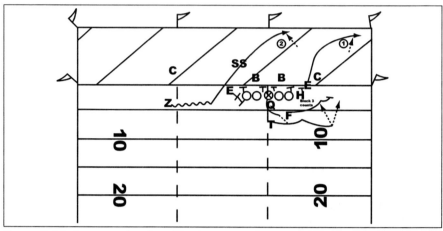

Figure 6-16. An example of a tailback pass against a goal line 6-2 defense

GOAL LINE

<u>RUNS</u>

STRONG WING LT 23 BLAST	STRONG WING RT 22 BLAST
HO WEAK WING RT 47 G LEAD	HO WEAK WING LT 46 G LEAD
WEAK WING RT LEAD OPTION LT	WEAK WING LT LEAD OPTION RT
UNBALANCED STRONG LT 47	UNBALANCED STRONG RT 46

<u>PASS</u>

HO WEAK WING RT 47 POWER PASS	HO WEAK WING LT 46 POWER PASS
WEAK WING RT 23 CROSS NAKED RT	WEAK WING LT 22 CROSS NAKED LT
STRONG I RT FAKE 22 BLAST SCISSORS	STRONG I LT FAKE 23 BLAST SCISSORS

Figure 6-17. An example of a game-plan, play call list for a goal line offense

Creating a Two-Point Play, Play Call Game Plan

Hypothetically, a team has just scored a touchdown, with only a few seconds remaining on the clock in the fourth quarter. It needs two points to tie the game and send the contest into overtime. Another possible scenario is that a team has just scored a touchdown, and its coaching staff has decided to forgo the possibility of going into overtime and instead has concluded to put it all on-the-line and "go for two" to win the game. This situation is no time for them to think "what should we call now?" Accordingly, as a part of their total red zone play call game plan, coaches must have two two-point plays ready to be called when the circumstances demand doing so.

In situations in which it might otherwise be argued that going for two points after a touchdown might be appropriate, coaches are faced with certain issues. For example, should both of the aforementioned two-point plays be passes? Should one be a pass and the other a run? Should both plays be two runs? Only the head coach and his staff can answer such questions. As a rule, the bottom line is that coaches should employ those plays that they have in their black zone and goal line arsenals that that believe will give their team the best chance of successfully converting the two-point plays from the three-yard line. A spread formation run-option play? A sprint-out run/pass option play? A dropback pass? A quick dropback pass or quick play-action pass? A special or trick play? Whatever the process for reaching a decision, the plays that they chose must be well-thought out, well-taught, well-coached, and well-practiced. This situation may be their team's last-ditch chance. As such, coaches must do everything in their power for their team to succeed in the pressure-filled two-point play situation.

What if the various game videos of their upcoming opponent's defense that the coaching staff broke down didn't include a two-point play situation? What should they do? Their initial step should be to look at video footage of other games of that opponent and see if it provides examples of the opponent's two-point play defense. If there are, the problem is addressed. If none exist, coaches should study their black zone and goal line breakdown videos and see how the opponent defenses the plays that the coaches are considering employing from the type of formations they are thinking of using.

Figure 6-18 provides an example of a two-point play game-plan, play call list. It should be noted that the actual horizontal placement of the football is marked for each of the two-point play, play calls. As such, when teams are going for a two-point play, they have one chance to get it right. Accordingly, teams want to be sure that the football is placed in the best horizontal-field position as possible—one that gives the offense its best chance of being successful. The quarterback must be well drilled in regard to knowing where such horizontal placement of the football should be on the three yard line and understand the mechanics of telling the referee where he wants the football placed for the two-point play try.

TWO-POINT PLAYS

ZOOM DOUBLE LT 140 HI-HO
BUNCH RT ZIP-ZAP FAKE 22 SPOT

Figure 6-18. An example of a two-point play game-plan, play call list

7

Practice Planning Wednesday's Play Call Game Plans

Hypothetically, it's mid-Wednesday morning. The coaching staff has just finished creating their red zone offense play call game-plan packages. At this point, their deep red zone, red zone, black zone, goal line, and, even, their two-point play packages are planned and ready to go. It's time to get to work on planning their Wednesday afternoon practice, which involves sitting down and planning their individual, unit, and team offensive practice-plan work so that they can be ready to execute their total play call, game plan in the red zone come game time.

Planning Off of a Daily Master Practice Plan

Just as they did for the planning of Tuesday's afternoon's practice, the key to sound practice planning for Wednesday is to work off of a constant, well-planned master daily-practice schedule. For Wednesday, as for any of their practice days, coaches start their practice-planning efforts by working off of a blank master daily-practice schedule, as was detailed in Figure 5-1. Given the fact that the team is in-season, coaches may be more apt to employ 21 periods of practice, or fewer. However, some coaches may believe in utilizing a longer, full two-hour, 24 period practice structure.

Practice in the Red Zone With Red-Zone Markers

No matter what the type of route, route combination, or pattern being utilized in the red zone, coaches must focus intently on their red zone, black zone, goal line, *and* two-point play route displacements. This factor is especially important because of the fact that as teams get closer and closer to the goal line, they have fewer and fewer vertical yards in which to work. This situation is why coaches tend to place so much teaching and coaching time helping their players to understand the importance of four key field markers: the sidelines, the end line, the goal line, and the six end zone pylon markers. The six pylon markers are placed on the two sideline-goal line intersections. In turn, the two sideline-end line intersections and the two pylons positioned on the end line are in line with the field hash marks. All coaches should realize that it is essential that players understand the significance of all of the end-zone line markings and the six pylons of the end zone. Such an understanding can enhance their ability to be better able to successfully execute many of their team's red zone, black zone, goal line, and two-point play pass routes, route combinations, and pass patterns. The field markings and flag-pylon positioning are illustrated in Figure 7-1.

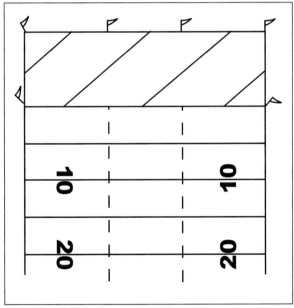

Figure 7-1. An illustration of the field markings and flag-pylon concept of the red zone

It is very important to note that *whenever* teams practice *any* type of red zone, black zone, goal line, or two-point play work, it is essential that they make sure to go down to the appropriate areas of the field to practice. This step is critical so that they can practice the skills, techniques, routes, route combinations, and pass patterns with all of the specific field/end-zone markings, as well as the cones or actual game-type pylons that they will encounter come game time. Coaches do this procedure to help create a truly game-like practice-type of environment in what is considered the four red zone situation areas.

If coaches are conducting a pre-practice, walk-through drill for their black zone offense, they should actually go down to the black zone area of their practice field to perform the drill, with all of the proper line markers and pylon placements. In a similar vein, if coaches schedule a 10-minute period for a red zone, one-on-one pass drill against the defense, the drill is started on the 20-yard line for red zone one-on-one work and then subsequently moved down closer to the red zone, black zone, and goal line areas as appropriate, as part of the same drill work. Furthermore, if the schedule calls for a red zone, black zone, or goal line 7-on-7 skeleton pass drill, coaches will be sure to go down to the appropriate area of the practice field to work in as a game-like environment as possible.

The same factor is also true for any two-point play practice. Since the goal line offense has their choice of horizontal positioning of the football on a two-point play try from hash to hash, coaches must be sure to place the football accordingly. In fact, coaches should do everything they can to practice in as realistic a game-like situation as possible.

Planning Wednesday's Unit and Team Practice Periods

Figure 7-2 details an overall base daily-practice plan structure for a heavy Wednesday practice day. The offense's primary practice emphasis for Wednesday is red zone offense, which includes the deep red zone, the red zone, the black zone, the goal line, and two-point plays. It is important to note how the practice structures are ordered during the course of the practice periods. While somewhat of a sense exists in the overall base daily-practice plan structure illustrated in Figure 7-2 of progressions from individual to unit to team work, a substantial degree of practice flexibility and even a feeling of surprise and freshness is inherent in the overall base practice plan structure, as outlined in Figure 7-2.

A review of the overall preliminary practice-plan structure presented in Figure 7-2 indicates that the start of practice (periods #1 and #2) has a two-period teaching and coaching walk-through session that is allotted 10 minutes. In line with the practice-planning concept of flexibility, the coaching staff has to decide what the offense needs to work on to prepare for the next opponent. For example, work on extra focus on

Date:		Day:		Time:	
Pre-Practice:					
Period	**WR**	**QB**	**RB**	**TE**	**OL**
1	Walk-Through Drills (Blitz Pick-Up Vs. Scouts)				
2					
3	Individual Run	Individual Run	Individual Run	Individual Run	Individual Run
4					
5	Team Run vs. Defense				
6					
7	Special Teams				
8					
9	Individual Pass	Individual Pass	Individual Pass	Individual Pass	Individual Pass
10					
11	1-on-1 Red Zone Pass Drill				1-on-1 Pass Pro vs. Def.
12					
13	Unit Red Zone 7-on-7 Skel. Pass Drill vs. Def.				Twist Pass Pass Pro vs. Def.
14					
15	Special Teams				
16	Team Red Zone Blitz Pick-Up vs. Scouts				
17					
18	Team Red Zone/Black Zone Offense vs. Scouts				
19					
20	Team Goal Line Off/Two Point Play vs. Scouts				
21					

Figure 7-2. An example of an overall base practice plan-structure for Wednesday

protection against the opponent's blitz pressure game by designating the walk-through drill as an extra blitz pick-up drill (at walk-through tempo). In this instance, the scout squad could be utilized to execute blitz after blitz in a rapid-style fashion.

The key point to remember, given the aforementioned scenario, is that a well thought-out practice script helps the offensive line and the backs to practice over and over all of the key frontal stunts and secondary blitzes that they could possibly encounter in their next game. Furthermore, the script should allow the quarterback to make all of his calls and possible checks at the line of scrimmage.

The walk-through period is essentially an on-the-field meeting, in which a virtual simulation (at a walking pace) occurs of assignments and techniques against potential on-the-field defensive problems, without either the offense or the defense being subjected to intense, demanding physical contact. Once properly organized and scripted, this drill can be utilized in a walk-through capacity at any time, including all the way up to a few hours before game time. Much of effective blitz pick-up is assignment, recognition, communication, and twist-type or cross-type exchange pick-ups. All of these factors can be facilitated and accomplished by performing such a blitz pick-up walk-through drill.

Periods #3 and #4 (10 minutes collectively) are assigned to individual coaching periods for teaching, coaching, drilling, and practicing the individual-position skills and techniques involved in the run game. This schedule is different from Tuesday's designation of Periods #3 and #4 being used for special teams practice. Most coaches use two of their team's four planned individual periods at this point of the practice rather than for special teams work in order to incorporate some variety into their practice schedule. In other words, the individual skills and techniques that will be needed for the run game are practiced in these two periods. The efforts undertaken in these two periods also serve to lead into the next two periods (periods #5 and #6) for the team run drill.

At this point, coaches have the option of either of the two extra periods for either a unit or a team drill for their team run drill. Similar to the unit, 9-on-7 inside-run drill, the team run drill for most coaches is one of the key, physical drills that they use to get their base, par down run game ready for their upcoming opponent. As in the unit, 9-on-7 inside-run drill, the team run drill is not executed against scout-squad players. Instead, the drill pits the first-team and second-team offenses and defenses against one another in whatever combination the head coach or the coordinators decide.

Just as in the unit, 9-on-7 inside-run drill, the offensive and defensive coordinators work together on the scripting of the drill so that both the offense and defense get good work against one another, rather than working against the scout-squad for all practice. Whenever possible, the offense and defense will employ those portions of their offense and defense that are similar to what their next opponent is going to utilize come game day to help make the drill as relevant as possible to prepare for their upcoming opponent.

In reality, the team run drill could easily be called the 11-on-11 run drill, because that is exactly what it is. A full team offense is going to work against a full team defense in a thud (non-scrimmage/non-tackling) context. The major difference between the team run drill and the unit, 9-on-7 inside-run drill is that the team run drill includes wide receivers to block secondary run-support defenders. The wide receivers can block safeties either from outside-in or head-up on inside runs. The wide receivers can then block safeties or cornerbacks inside-out to head-up on outside runs.

The other basic difference between the two drills is that where the unit, 9-on-7 inside-run drill focuses on inside-run plays, runs in the team run drill can be targeted to either the inside or the outside. Another major difference between the two drills is that in the team run drill, coaches often incorporate two to three play action passes in order to try to keep the defense more honest in their efforts against both the run and the pass game. This step also allows the offense to work on their coordinated run and play-action pass package. An example of a team run drill is presented in Figure 7-3.

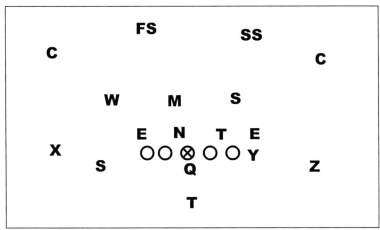

Figure 7-3. An example of a team run drill

Periods #7 and #8, also collectively for a 10-minute segment, are allotted to the practice of special teams games. Subsequently, periods #9 and #10 (10 minutes total) are two additional sessions that are assigned as individual coaching periods. Since the prior two periods of individual coaching have already been utilized for the run game, these two other planned individual periods are designated for the teaching, coaching, and practicing of individual pass-game skills and techniques.

Similar to what was done with the run game, practicing the pass game is undertaken in a most basic form, by working on the appropriate skills and techniques involved in the pass game with individual practice periods. Figure 7-1 illustrates two individual pass-emphasis periods (#9 and #10), which lead into the unit, 1-on-1, red zone pass-drill periods (#11 and #12). Simultaneously, the offensive line engages in a unit, 1-on-1, pass pro drill with the defensive line. Teams then go into their unit, red zone, 7-on-7 skeleton-pass drill periods (#13 and #14), while the offensive line performs a unit, twist pass pro, pick-up drill against the defensive line.

For Wednesday's practice, the key practice-plan focus for the day is red zone offense. As a result, coaches will not, necessarily, worry about third-down situations. Instead, periods #11 and #12 are dedicated to performing a unit, 1-on-1 pass drill in the red zone, which makes the drill a unit, 1-on-1 red zone pass drill. The offense then practices their specific red zone routes from on or inside of the 20-yard line against 1-on-1 red zone coverage.

The drill is conducted from different places on the field. For example, the drill might start on the left hash for three minutes, on the 18-yard line. The drill, then, might be performed in the middle of the field for three minutes, from the 12-yard line. The final three to four minutes might then involve operating the drill from the right hash on the six-yard line in the black zone. In fact, every time teams perform this drill, they usually will change the hash-mark and yard-line parameters of the drill, so that both the offensive and the defensive players will have the opportunity to practice their 1-on-1 pass skills throughout varied locations in both the red zone and black zone areas.

Periods #13 and #14 are reserved for conducting the unit, red zone 7-on-7, pass-skeleton drill, which is consistent with the underlying key practice-plan focus for Wednesday—red zone offense. In this situation, the offense practices its specific red zone pass offense in the red zone against the defense's red zone defensive coverages.

The format of the practice can vary from team to team. For example, practice could start with four repetitions from the deep red zone on the 32-yard line. The football could then be placed in the red zone at the 19-yard line for four repetitions, and then, perhaps, at the 12-yard line for four more repetitions. The drill could be completed with the final four repetitions on the seven-yard line in the black zone. In all of the various yardage situations, it is essential that the positioning of the football with regard to the hash mark and middle of the field be varied.

Period #15 is an additional session that is devoted to special team practice, if only for five minutes. As has already been discussed, forcing the offense and defense to run on the field for a last-minute, field-goal attempt and subsequent field-goal block can be an excellent way to use a relatively brief block of special teams' practice time. Interjecting a special teams period in the middle of a practice to work on onside kicking can help to add variety to practice, as well as be a viable means of breaking up the daily practice plan that is often the same, or almost the same, every day.

As on Tuesday's practice, Periods #16 to #21 (30 minutes of practice time in all) are the end point of what all of the individual and unit drills and practice work to that point have been building up to—team periods against the scout squad. Figure 7-1 illustrates that the team periods target the major game-planning concept of the day—red zone offense, just as the previous periods on Wednesday's practice already have. The team periods work on all of the team's deep red zone, red zone, black zone, goal line, and two-point play game-plan play calls.

In addition, a special, two-period block of time (Periods #16 and #17) is assigned to prepare for the strong possibility of needing an effective blitz pick-up in the red zone. Practicing the actual red zone offense game-plan plays is undertaken in periods #18 and #19, a schedule that may include any deep red zone plays, as well as black zone play calls on which coaches may want to work. Periods #20 and #21 are allotted to the practice of goal line game-plan plays, including any predetermined two-point play calls.

At this point, coaches usually work on their play-call scripting, targeting what they feel their opponent's red zone defense will likely do to defense them in each of the critical red zone areas and play-call situations (e.g., deep red zone, red zone, black zone, goal line. and two-point plays). Coaches take great efforts to organize and conduct red zone practice that is as game-like as possible for what they expect to encounter come game day against their opponent.

A practice-plan tactic that many coaches like to use is to save one period of the practice for a surprise critical situation involving both the offense and defense or one for the kicking game. Hypothetically, at the end of a practice period, the head coach could, suddenly, blow on his whistle, place the football on the plus three-yard line, and announce that the offense has three chances to attempt a two-point conversion. "If the offense scores twice, there will be no after-practice run conditioning for the offense. On the other hand, if the defense can make two, two-point conversion stops, no running for the defense. Scrimmage situation … stay off the quarterback."

When such an event takes place, both the offense and defense have to switch gears from whatever drill situation they were just practicing and immediately find a way to "rev up their motor and get after the opposition." Why would coaches use such an unexpected, unscheduled practice tactic? First of all, such a sudden-change tactic could help both the offense and the defense to learn how to immediately focus on some aspect of a game-like critical situation that *must* be successfully handled … right now. It can also be a great change-of-pace practice tactic that could help to break practice plan staleness and monotony. In addition, and, perhaps, most importantly, it can help to promote *competition*. It's very difficult to win without having intense competitors on the team. Some teams are very fortunate to have natural, fierce competitors on their teams. Most teams, however, have to find ways to develop such competitors. A sudden switch to a highly competitive two-point play conversion scrimmage, in the middle of practice with no warning, can do a lot to help develop a highly competitive spirit in the entire team. Furthermore, such a tactic can help coaches to practice the kind of change-of-pace action that is often involved in a sudden critical-situation that can occur during the game. This factor can be especially true for the play caller.

Put Wednesday's Play Call Game Plan on Boards in Staff Room

Just as they did on Tuesday, at this point, coaches should put all of their specific red zone play call game plans on the blank play call charts on the boards in their offensive staff room. In addition, they should also enter their red zone plan in their computer as they continue to make progress completing their actual weekly game-plan play list. As noted previously, their red zone offense plan consists of all their deep red zone, red zone, black zone, and two-point play, play call ideas.

Creating Wednesday's Practice-Period Scripts

In reality, developing practice-period scripts for Wednesdays is no different than creating practice scripts for Tuesdays, except for one major variation. As they normally do, coaches compile a list (order) of plays that they would like to work on in the limited amount time that they have to practice the various designated, predetermined, game-like situations. The major deviation to their scripting efforts on Wednesdays is the focus on red zone practice, whenever possible.

To a degree, they may have already addressed this issue in some of their unit drills, for example, a red zone 1-on-1 pass drill or a red zone 7-on-7 skeleton-pass drill. Initially, they might perform a few repetitions of these drills in the deep red zone (hypothetically on the 33-yard line, for example). Then, they might move to the 18-yard line to get several repetitions in the red zone, before shifting to the seven-yard line for some repetitions in the black zone. As they move closer and closer to the goal line, since they remain concerned with hash-mark considerations, they continue to consider both vertical and lateral field factors.

When coaches get to their normal, team, red zone practice periods (periods #18 to #21 detailed in Figure 7-2), they tend to do everything that they can to enact actual red zone drives. Figure 7-4 outlines a red zone drive script, starting in the deep red zone and moving next into the red zone for periods #18 and #19. A similar script would then be made to practice black zone, goal line, and two-point play needs for periods #20 and #21. Coaches should employ down-and-distance markers so that every practice-play repetition is as realistically game-like as possible.

Over the course of four periods, many coaches believe that they should be able to get off a minimum of 26 plays. On the other hand, many coaches will keep their first and second offensive units out on the field for a complete red zone drive, starting in the deep red zone and working all the way down to two two-point play tries. As a rule, in this situation, the first offense will execute a complete drive of approximately 13 plays (two deep red zone, four red zone, five black zone/goal line, and two two-point plays). When the first offense finishes their drive, the second offense then repeats the same red zone script. More often than not, many teams adhere to this concept on both Thursday and Friday, given the fact that it has such a substantial perceived game-like practice value.

Scripting Team Scripts

Since teams start out in periods #1 and #2 with a special emphasis on performing a normal walk-through drill on Wednesday, they often change the coach to which the script is assigned. For example, if teams have decided to use the walk-through drill for an extra blitz pick-up drill, they will earmark their offensive line coach to script the walk-through, blitz pick-up drill. Such an appointment will assure him that his charges will have the opportunity to practice their blitz pick-up skills and techniques against the defensive-blitz for which he feels that they most need to prepare.

Date:			Practice: Tuesday		Periods: 16 & 17	Drill: Team base, par down offense
#	H	D & D	Per	Formation	Play Call	Defense
1	L	1-10 +35	11 (1 off)	Doubles Lt	246 Double Post	43 Over Saw – 0
2	M	1-10 +30	11 (1 off)	Doubles Rt	5 Revese Double Pass QB	43 Cross Buck — 1
3	R	1-10 +20	10 (1 off)	Dixie Rt	247 Smash	43 Under – Q
4	R	2-5 +15	12 (1 off)	Ho Wing Lt	47	43 Over – 2
5	RM	3-2 +12	12 (1 off)	Str Rt Tite Z In	12 Blast	Bear – 1
6	LM	4-1 +11	20 (1 off)	Split Slot Rt	Crack Option Lt	6-1 Double Go – 1
7	R	1-10 +20	10 (2 off)	Dixie Rt	247 Smash	4-3 Under – Q
8	R	2-5 +15	12 (2 off)	Ho Wing Lt	47	4-3 Over – Z
9	RM	3-2 +12	12 (2 off)	Str Rt Tite Z In	12 Blast	Bear – 1
10	LM	4-1 +11	20 (2 off)	Split Slot Rt	Crack Option Lt	6-1 Double Go – 1
11	R	1-10 +20	11 (1 off)	Trey Lt Socket	21 Trap	40 Double TE – Q
12	M	2-7 +17	21 (1 off)	Weak Lt Across	79 Y Delay	3-3 Stack – 3
13	L	3-4 +14	11 (1 off)	Double Lt	90 Slant	4-3 Field Blitz – 3

Figure 7-4. An example of a red zone drive script (deep red zone and red zone)

Furthermore, the offensive line coach, usually the run-game expert on an offensive staff, knows that each week, he should expect to be assigned the responsibility of scripting the unit, 9-on-7, inside-run period or the team run drill (also referred to as the 11-on-11 run drill), whichever has been decided upon for each particular "heavy day" practice. For the example of a practice-plan structure, detailed in Figure 7-2, the draft illustrates a degree of flexibility in the team's practice planning that enables an adjustment in practice needs to be undertaken, either in general or for a specific upcoming opponent. As a result, two team-type periods have been substituted for two unit-type periods. During periods #5 and #6, for example, a team run drill is scheduled instead of a unit, 9-on-7, inside-run drill. On the other hand, in this situation, coaches don't necessarily have to treat the team run drill in a red zone context, which is the practice theme of the day. Instead, the focus for this drill is a base run-game emphasis, with the offense and the defense working against one another, just as they did in Tuesday's unit, 9-on-7, inside-run drill. As before, both the offensive and defensive staffs cooperate with one another in an effort to get the offense's run attack and the defense's run stop capabilities ready for Saturday's upcoming opponent.

As a rule, coaches don't script their 1-on-1, red zone pass drill. On the other hand, if they did, or felt it necessary to do so, they would assign the scripting to their wide receiver coach. With the inherent variations of route running in the deep red zone, red zone, black zone, and goal line, as well as employing special routes used only in red zone areas, most coaches tend to think that their wide receiver coach is the most qualified person on the staff to develop a 1-on-1, red zone, pass-drill script. More often than not, they also believe that their wide receiver coach is the best individual to act as their red zone pass-game expert. As a result, he is typically assigned to script the red zone, 7-on-7, skeleton-pass drill periods (#13 and #14).

The offensive coordinator handles the scripting of the team red zone blitz pick-up periods (#16 and #17). Most head coaches feel that since the red zone blitz threat and blitz pick-up are of such extreme importance, both of these periods should be overseen by the offensive coordinator. When coaches get to the team red zone practice against the scout team (periods #18 and #19), scripting both practice segments is assigned to their offensive backfield coach. As such, the run game is of such great importance in this area of the field that it makes sense for teams to utilize their offensive backfield coach as their goal line expert. Furthermore, since the offensive backs are such a big part of most team's blitz pick-up package, having the offensive backfield coach as the periods' scripter seems to be particularly appropriate. As discussed previously, when teams get to the team goal line offense period and two-point play period (#20 and #21 respectively), against the scout team, their tight end coach (their goal line expert) is often considered to be the best choice for handling their scripting.

8

Putting the Finishing Touches on the Situational Game Plans

Hypothetically, again, it's now Wednesday evening, and the staff is back from dinner. They've reviewed the practice video from Wednesday afternoon's practice. They've analyzed their red zone offense package to see what they might need to add, drop, or tweak. For the remainder of the evening, they start to put the finishing touches on the situational game plans that still need attention—their coming-out offense; their four-minute, slow-slow offense; and their two-minute, hurry-hurry offense.

Coming-Out Offense

One extremely critical game situation is coming-out offense. One of the toughest offensive situations is for a team to be backed up to its own goal line, behind the five-yard line. Failure in this offensive zone of the field will, most likely, put its opponent in an extremely favorable position to score. In this situation, a primary goal of most coaches is to get two first downs so that they can move the ball into what is commonly referred to as the play-it zone, beyond the offense's 20-yard line. Once in the play-it zone, the offense will have a much greater degree of freedom to utilize all, or at least most, of its base offense.

In order to get two first downs, the offense must obviously gain an initial first down. Being backed up to the goal line can make this task an extremely difficult chore. Quite often, most defenses, like sharks smelling blood in the water, will pressure a backed-up offense. The defense knows not only that it has a reasonable opportunity to make a tackle in the end zone that will give it a two-point safety, it also can provide its offense with excellent field position after the opposition's kick—safety or not. As a result, the offense is frequently forced into an anti-pressure mode.

A number of coaches believe that the primary goal of a coming-out offense is to at least punch the ball out to the four-yard line so that the offense can utilize its spread-punt formation if it can't convert a first down. As such, the offense wants to ensure enough room for their spread-punt kicking game. They don't want the punt team to have to use a tight-punt formation and put extra pressure on their punter, who would be closer to the line of scrimmage than normal and crammed back against the end line of the end zone.

Other coaches have a philosophy that is contrary to the aforementioned reasoning. Instead, they want to attack the defense in the coming-out zone, much as they do on any area of the field. Gaining a first down is their main goal. If they can't, they then want to make sure that they gain enough yardage to allow them to employ a spread-punt formation.

In reality, a number of sound philosophies exist regarding what to do when the offense is backed up against its own goal line. Some coaches prefer to utilize their very best plays in this situation, regardless of whether the plays are runs or passes. On the other hand, some coaches might want to employ a power offense, bringing in extra tight end/fullback personnel to grind out needed yardage, similar to their thought process for their goal line offense. An option offense, for example, might continue to utilize the option plays that it normally uses; even though many coaches feel pitching the ball to the back who is in the end zone can be extremely dangerous.

Personally, my coming-out offensive philosophy is to use safe formations and utilize our best straight-ahead runs, quick passes, and quick play-action passes. Furthermore, through the use of our various formations, we want to ensure that there are no, or few at most, short edges (i.e., no tight-end alignments) that would enable the defense to create havoc with edge-rush pressure. Employing our most efficient, straight ahead-hitting run plays helps us to avoid negative-yardage runs. Avoiding negative-yardage runs is a key element of a successful coming-out offense, particularly since it minimizes the likelihood of giving up a safety. As a result, counter-run plays and reverses have a lower priority in our coming-out offense play call list. It should also be noted that our quarterback always has to be ready to execute a sneak, in case the football is positioned inside of the one-yard line, a situation in which a need exists for more "breathing room," in order for us to be able to enact our more basic, coming-out offensive plays.

If the defense tries to load up on the run, we can not be afraid to throw the football, especially with our quick-pass game. We also believe that our quick play-action pass game can be very effective in this situation. On the other hand, we are very careful about using bootleg or sprint-out type of pass action, even though many coaches feel quite comfortable utilizing such play calls as a part of their coming-out offense package. Our primary concern, just as it would be on a sweep or option-pitch play, is whether to put the football in the hands of a ballcarrier on bootlegs and sprint-out passes deeply off the line of scrimmage, relatively close to or in the end zone, which could possibly result in a safety.

A big part of our coming-out philosophy is to be sure to *go on the attack*. As such, we believe that we will get that needed first down and will find a way to do it. On the other hand, coming-out offense is not a situation that coaches should take lightly. To us, it is another critical game situation that we *must* win in order to help us succeed in the game that we are playing. While we want to be sure to be smart with our play calling, we certainly don't want to be overly conservative with it either. Employing a play call list of run, run, pass is not our approach in the coming-out zone. Rather, our coming-out offense play call plans are based on what plays we believe will give us our best chance of succeeding—run or pass.

Creating a Coming-Out Offense Play Call Game Plan

In reality, creating a coming-out offense game plan can often be a bit of a guessing game on occasion. For example, a team might be facing an opponent for the week that might have already played five or six games of the season and, yet, never has been in a situation involving a coming-out defense. How can coaches study video of that team's coming-out defense? Quite frankly, they can't. In another example, a team's upcoming opponent may have been in a coming-out defense just once up to that point of the season, a situation in which they employed an aggressive, attacking, blitzing coming-out defense play call plan. In reality, it might have employed such a defensive tactic that week in the coming-out zone, primarily because its opponent was extremely weak at handling pressuring, blitzing defenses. On the other hand, it might have great respect for another opponent's abilities to handle blitz pressure and might utilize a conservative coming-out defensive philosophy, as a result. As a consequence, coaches are in somewhat of a dilemma concerning what they should do for a coming-out offense play call game plan.

As a rule, when creating their coming-out offense play call game plan, coaches should adhere to their basic coming-out offense philosophy. Formationally, they should try to not give the defense short corners (i.e., no tight ends) or, at a minimum, not give it very many. Coaches should run the football north-south, keeping in mind to employ run plays that help to ensure no negative-yardage plays. Furthermore, coaches should throw quick, using their quick, three-step dropback pass game, as well as their quick play-action passes.

At that point, they might also incorporate an additional run or pass play that they feel can be very effective against that specific opponent. Could they also employ a special, or trick, play? Certainly, they could and would if they thought that their opponent's coming-out defense might be vulnerable to such a play. In reality, they could use any play, for example, a counter-run or a counter-pass play, in their coming-out arsenal that they felt reasonably certain could be safely executed in the coming-out zone.

Figure 8-1 provides an example of a coming-out offense game-plan, play call list. It should be noted that the plan is purposefully not very lengthy. Coaches who conduct an end-of-season study will probably find that they would only be in this critical situation a handful of times over the course of the season. As such, they will employ their best, most effective plays and execute them out of what they believe to be the most appropriate formations for those particular run or pass plays. In addition, if their team is better running its off-tackle power play to the left, then that's the way it will run it in this critical coming-out offense situation. As such, this factor would also apply to any other play in a team's coming-out offense arsenal.

COMING-OUT OFFENSE

<u>RUNS</u>

ACE RT SNEAK RT   ACE LT SNEAK LT
STRONG LT ZIP-ZAP 47   STRONG RT ZIP-ZAP 46
ACE RT 22/23 CHECK-WITH-ME   ACE LT 22/23 CHECK-WITH-ME
WING LT TWINS HO-HUM 23 LEAD   WING RT TWINS HO-HUM 22 LEAD
WING RT RETURN 24 FORCE   WING LT RETURN 25 FORCE

<u>PASS</u>

ACE RT 90 HITCH   ACE LT 90 HITCH
ZOOM DOUBLES LT 93   ZOOM DOUBLES RT 93
ZOOM STRONG WING RT TITE FAKE 22 FLOOD   ZOOM STRONG WING LT TITE FAKE 23 FLOOD

Figure 8-1. An example of a coming-out offense game-plan, play call list

Four-Minute, Slow-Slow Offense

Hypothetically, 4:43 remains on the game clock in the fourth quarter and a team has a two-point lead. Its opponent has just punted the football to them, so the situation is first-and-ten on its own 18-yard line. Its opponent has two time-outs left. At this point, the goal of the offense is to use up the remaining time on the clock, employing what many coaches refer to as the four-minute, slow-slow offense. Truth be known, the time remaining on the clock could be 3:43 or 5:43, it doesn't really matter. The offense is in a situation where it needs to use up the time on the clock by maintaining possession of the football. The game must end without the opposition having another opportunity to score and win the game. In the vernacular of football slang, it's now time to "grind meat." The offense wants to run the football to use up the clock and go home a winner. They want to run the football, all-the-while keeping the football in-bounds, so that the clock is not stopped and restarted on the ensuing snap.

Much like red zone offense game-plan, play call efforts, the four-minute, slow-slow offense play call game plan should be condensed and tight. In reality, definite similarities exist between red zone offense and four-minute, slow-slow offense. In both situations, the defense is normally very stressed. Failure in the red zone can result in giving up three or seven points. Failure in four-minute, slow-slow defense can mean the loss of a game.

Similar to coming-out offense, the offensive coaching staff may have very few opportunities to study game video of the defense of their upcoming opponent facing four-minute, slow-slow offense situations. As a result, the offense may not be aware of exactly what it should prepare for. In this situation, studying its opponent's pressuring red zone defense may very well be its best bet. In both cases, the defense is in a very difficult situation, feeling that it has to make something happen to stop the offense and produce a turnover.

No matter what type of run or pass play will be utilized during a team's four-minute, slow-slow offense, certain key factors and rules should be followed. For example, the quarterback must be sure, in his line of scrimmage snap-count mechanics, to use up as much time on the play clock as possible, before he barks out the call word that tells the center to snap the ball. Another basic factor is that whoever is running with the ball must keep it in-bounds so that the clock is not stopped and restarted on the ensuing snap. In other words, ballcarriers *must* be sure to be tackled in-bounds. The third guideline in this situation is that the offensive players should unpile slowly once the ballcarrier is tackled to the ground. As such, the offensive players should get off the pile of offenders and defenders slowly, one-by-one, as if they were layers of an onion being peeled off one at a time. All affected offenders should move as slowly as the officials will allow them in order to burn every second off the clock as possible.

Kill-the-clock offense, which should be used once there are not enough seconds left on the clock in combination with the amount of time-outs the opposition has, is a big part of the four-minute, slow-slow offense philosophy of many coaches. In reality, it has the same targeted goal that four-minute, slow-slow offense has. Most teams usually work on their kill-the-clock offense on their light, Friday practices. As such, additional information on kill-the-clock offense is presented in Chapters 10 and 11.

Four-Minute, Slow-Slow Offense Play Call Game Plan

Formationing is an essential underlying concept for four-minute, slow-slow offense. This factor can be particularly true for the run game. For example, two and three tight end/H-back/fullback-types can help to eliminate short edges in efforts by the defense to bring edge pressures. In addition, such extra tight end/H-back/fullback-types can also help to provide extra power-type blocking at the run points of attack to combat any defensive overloads that might exist. On the other hand, the offense can also utilize extra tight ends/H-backs/fullback-types to produce overloaded formations of its own to combat extra secondary safety or cornerback run support. One of the problems with such reasoning is that tightened offensive formations almost always result in tightened, condensed defensive alignments, which makes the defense harder to run against.

The underlying basis for the four-minute slow-slow offense run-game reasoning of most coaches is to utilize their best, most efficient run plays. The two sources from which they initially attempt to identify effective new plays to incorporate in their four-minute slow-slow offense are their base, par down run play call list and their red zone run play call list. As a rule, coaches prefer to use north-south type run plays that have a limited likelihood of resulting in negative yardage. While, on occasion, they will employ outside-run plays that can gain valuable outside run-game yardage, they want to be certain that a running back, on an outside-run course, has the ability to run with the football and still have the chance to purposely fall, or dive, to the ground before going out of bounds. Run-option plays can be very effective in this situation, especially if a team's offense is built around run-option offense. On the other hand, run-option plays executed from the hash marks into the boundary can often force the pitch back to receive a pitch and then run out of bounds before he has a chance to down himself on the field of play.

The four-minute slow-slow offense can be an excellent situation to consider using counter- and reverse-run action. Quarterback bootleg or naked bootleg keeper-actions can also be very effective against hard-flowing defensive fronts. The key point to remember about this possibility is that the counter/reverse ballcarrier or the keeping bootleg quarterback must always remember to stay in-bounds and slide or dive to the ground in order to help keep the clock moving. Running out of bounds must be avoided at almost all costs, unless it means getting a first down and a fresh, new set of downs.

Passing the football is also a distinct possibility for four-minute slow-slow offense, especially given the potential of the defense to try to tighten down its alignments to stop the run. The main problem in this situation is, of course, the fact that an incomplete pass stops the clock—a circumstance that the offense wants to definitely avoid. If, however, the defense tries to overload the front to put eight or nine defenders in the box, throwing quick, three-step drop passes can help provide the vital yardage necessary to gain first-down yardage, move the chains, and gain additional plays that can eat up the remaining time on the clock. Counter passes, such as bootlegs, naked bootlegs, and waggle passes can be very effective against defensive fronts that, at this point of the game, tend to be desperately pursuing the fast flow of the football.

On such misdirection, play-action passing, the mindset of the quarterback should be on executing keeper-runs, as much as he may be actually thinking about passing the football. If his intended receiver is wide open, the gamble involved in throwing has a reasonably high chance of succeeding to help produce a first down. On the other hand, if any doubt exists as to whether his receiver is well covered or not, the quarterback should think *keep* the ball and turn himself into the a ballcarrier, rather than risking an interception or an incompletion. Figure 8-2 presents an example of a four-minute slow-slow offense play call game plan.

```
┌─────────────────────────────────────────────────────────────────────────┐
│                    FOUR-MINUTE SLOW-SLOW OFFENSE                          │
│                                                                           │
│                                RUNS                                       │
│                                                                           │
│  SWITCH UNBALANCED STRONG RT 22 LEAD     SWITCH UNBALANCED STRONG LT 23 LEAD
│  TRADE WEAK LT ZOOM 37 COUNTER           TRADE WEAK RT ZOOM 36 COUNTER     │
│  ACE RT OVER 22/23 CHECK-WITH-ME         ACE LT OVER 22/23 CHECK-WITH-ME   │
│  SHIFT UNBALANCED RT 46                  SHIFT UNBALANCED LT 47            │
│  DOUBLES RT S FLY 46                     DOUBLES LT S FLY 47              │
│  ACE RT 22/23 CHECK-WITH-ME              ACE LT 22/23 CHECK-WITH-ME       │
│  ZOOM STRONG PRO RT SWEEP RT             ZOOM STRONG PRO LT SWEEP LT      │
│  I RT ZIN 32 BELLY                       I LT ZIN 33 BELLY                │
│  STRONG RT 24 FORCE NAKED LT KEEPER      STRONG LT 25 FORCE NAKED RT KEEPER
│                                                                           │
│                                PASS                                       │
│                                                                           │
│  ACE RT 90 HITCH                         ACE LT 90 HITCH                  │
│  TRADE TREY RT 90 DOUBLE IN              TRADE TREY LT 90 DOUBLE IN       │
│  DOUBLES LT 245 SLOT CROSS               DOUBLES RT 145 SLOT CROSS        │
│  STRONG PRO RT 90 ROLLS F ANGLE          STRONG PRO RT 90 ROLLS F ANGLE   │
└─────────────────────────────────────────────────────────────────────────┘
```

Figure 8-2. An example of a four-minute slow-slow offense play call game plan

Two-Minute Hurry-Hurry Offense

In another hypothetical situation, less than two minutes are left in the game. Your team is behind by two points and needs 45 yards to get into legitimate field-goal range for its field goal kicker. Another potential scenario is that the team is behind by five or six points and needs a touchdown to win the game, with 80 yards to go. Another hypothetical key situation that seems to occur often is that it is the end of the first half, and the team has a chance to increase its point total before it goes into the locker room. In all of these circumstantial settings, the two-minute, hurry-hurry offense will be an extremely critical, often pressure-filled facet of a team's offensive game plan, a situation in which success or failure will depend on whether a team can score points (or not).

Like any other critical offensive situation, whether a team's two-minute, hurry-hurry offense is pressure-filled will be a function of whether it is well-planned and well-practiced. An effective two-minute, hurry-hurry offense is well-designed. The players, although they normally will not have the two-minute, hurry-hurry play call plan memorized, should feel comfortable when a two-minute, hurry-hurry play call is made. The way players respond to every critical-situation offensive situation should be characterized by hustle and confidence, not by being harried and frantic. In addition, a well-oiled, well-drilled, two-minute, hurry-hurry offense relies on sound communication at the line of scrimmage when the clock is not stopped and the offense cannot take the time to huddle up.

Two-minute, hurry-hurry offense actually has two distinct parts to it. The hurry-hurry aspect refers to the fact that the clock is running, and the offense does not have the time to huddle-up to make a play call. Instead, via whatever cadence, on-the-line play call system an offense uses, the play calls are made at the line of scrimmage. An effective key for the hurry-hurry part of the two-minute offense is that only one, or two at most, offensive formations are utilized. This step is undertaken for the sake of familiarity and simplicity. For example, a basic quarterback call of "on-the-line, doubles right … on-the line, doubles right," once to each side of the field, should, simply and efficiently, get the offense to the line of scrimmage in the desired formation.

Many teams require their receivers to stay on their respective side of the field during the on-the-line, hurry-hurry stage of two-minute offense. As a result, the wide receiver to the left side of the field would stay on the left side of the field, while the wide receiver to the right side of the field would stay on the right side of the field during the on-the-line, hurry-hurry stage of the two-minute offense. Which receiver would stay on the line of scrimmage as the split end and which receiver would align off the line of scrimmage would then be determined by the quarterback's call. This measure is employed to save the wide receivers' legs from getting tired during such a pass-oriented situation by keeping them from having to run across the field to reset, because of a change-of-formation-side call.

Once the on-the-line, hurry-hurry formationing is set, the quarterback can call plays from a short list of a memorized hurry-hurry play call, game-plan list. More commonly, most quarterbacks look to the sideline to get an on-the-line, hurry-hurry play call signal from a coach or a player signaler. The other factor that can be undertaken is for the quarterback to look to the sideline to get a play call from a coach. The quarterback then barks out a play call to the wide receiver on each side of the line to ensure that everyone can hear the call.

The other distinct part of two-minute, hurry-hurry offense is huddle-up offense, which occurs when the clock is stopped and stays stopped until the ball is snapped for the next play. Such a situation could result from a number of reasons, for example, the football has been run out-of-bounds or a pass has fallen incomplete. In this circumstance, the coach play caller then makes a two-minute offense play call, which is either signaled in or sent in by a substitute player who serves as a messenger to the quarterback who is in huddle on the field.

Creating a Two-Minute, Hurry-Hurry Play Call Game Plan

As a result of the fact that two-minute, hurry-hurry offense typically has two distinct parts, most coaches actually create two relatively brief two-minute, hurry-hurry play call game plans. The first is the actual on-the-line, hurry-hurry play call game plan, which normally is a short, condensed list of plays. When the clock is running, all of the on-the-line, hurry-hurry play calls are signaled out to the quarterback because the offense is in an on-the-line status. Some teams also have an on-the-line, hurry-hurry play call game plan that has been created in the off-season. This particular play call game plan allows teams to practice the on-the-line, hurry-hurry part or their two-minute, hurry-hurry offense the first day of fall practices if they so desired.

The hurry-hurry plan is typically comprised of a team's most basic, quick, three-step dropback passes, five- and seven-step dropback passes, a few screens, one draw, and possibly one or two other run plays. Most teams almost never add to that list during a game-plan week. On the other hand, they will delete from that list any pass calls that they perceive will not be effective against the pass coverages that they are expecting to encounter from their opponent's two-minute, hurry-hurry defense. The same point would apply to any run play that the coaches feel would not be effective against their next opponent in this situation. Figure 8-3 provides an example of an on-the-line, hurry-hurry play call game plan.

ON-THE-LINE, HURRY-HURRY OFFENSE

<u>RUNS</u>

21 TRAP	20 TRAP
41 DRAW	42 DRAW
SPEED OPTION LT	SPEED OPTION RT

<u>PASS</u>

90 HITCH	90 HITCH
92 SLANT	90 SLANT
93 INSIDE	93 INSIDE
90 HITCH-GO	90 HITCH-GO
90 SLANT-GO	90 SLANT-GO
140 ACUTE	240 ACUTE
140 STREAKS	240 STREAKS
145 Y/S CROSS	245 Y/S CROSS
246 DOUBLE POST	146 DOUBLE POST
147 SMASH	247 SMASH

Figure 8-3. An example of an on-the-line, hurry-hurry offense play call game plan

As has been previously discussed, the other distinct part of two-minute, hurry-hurry offense is huddle-up offense, which occurs when the clock is stopped and stays stopped until the ball is snapped for the next play. In reality, a team's two-minute, hurry-hurry offense can take whatever normal time it needs to huddle-up, make player substitutions, and make play calls that are not on the hurry-hurry play call game plan. The primary advantage of this particular additional two-minute, hurry-hurry play call plan is that it allows for play calls from formations other than the ones utilized in the on-the-line, hurry-hurry offense game plan. One key concern with regard to having two separate play call plans is that whatever the personnel plans are for the huddle-up play call game plan, they must be the same as the ones used for the on-the-line, hurry-hurry, play call game plan. If an offense doesn't adhere to this stipulation, it will be imperative that the two-minute, hurry-hurry offense is coached well enough to make such personnel substitution changes "on the fly" from off the sideline.

Much like the on-the-line, hurry-hurry play call game-plan list, it is beneficial to keep the two-minute, huddle-up offense play call game-plan list tight and condensed. It should be remembered that the plays on the two-minute, huddle-up play call game-plan list are in addition to the on-the-line, hurry-hurry play call game-plan list.

One basic goal of coaches is to use pass plays that they feel will best attack their opponent's two-minute, hurry-hurry defense. For example, if from video study, they have a relatively good idea of what their opponent will do to defend a two-minute, hurry-hurry offense situation, they can zero in on attacking the anticipated defensive coverages with a fairly limited number of additional pass plays. On the other hand, if they're not sure what the opponent's defense will do in such a situation, they might decide to enlarge their pass plan, so that they are able to confidently and effectively attack a possibly greater variety of pass coverages.

Extensive video study may also allow coaches to be aware of the fact that a specific run play executed from a formation that is normally not employed in the on-the-line, hurry-hurry game plan may be of great value in the two-minute, hurry-hurry offense situation. As a result, the coaching staff could add this particular run play to their two-minute, huddle-up play call game plan. Figure 8-4 presents an example of a two-minute, huddle-up play call game plan.

HUDDLE-UP OFFENSE

<u>RUNS</u>

TRIPS LT ROLL RT SAIL	TRIPS RT ROLL LT SAIL
TRIPS LT SOLID 164 Z CLEAR	TRIPS RT SOLID 264 Z CLEAR
TREY RT 244 S CLEAR	TREY LT 144 S CLEAR
GUN TREY RT 140 ALLEY	GUN TREY LT 240 ALLEY
DOUBLES LT 145Y X-DIG	DOUBLES RT 245Y X-DIG
TREY RT 240 Y READ	THREY LT 140 Y READ

Figure 8-4. An example of a two-minute, huddle-up play call game plan

Practice Planning Thursday's Play Call Game Plans

Hypothetically, it's now Thursday morning and the coaching staff has just finished putting the finishing touches on their situational game plans for their coming-out offense, their four-minute, slow-slow offense, and their two-minute, hurry-hurry offense. It's time to get to work on planning their Thursday afternoon practice. Since Thursday is a shortened, light, no-padded practice day, they sit down and plan team-only, offensive practice plan work against the scout squad. Some coaches also prefer to practice their two-minute, hurry-hurry offense against their own defense, rather than their scout squad, in order to get faster, more challenging work for both sides of the football. Practicing these three major game-plan concerns, in addition to a few other key practice touch-up needs, allows teams to get very close to being ready to execute their total play call game plan, come game time.

Planning Off of a Daily Master Practice Plan

Similar to the planning of Tuesday and Wednesday afternoon's practice, the key to sound practice planning for Thursday is to plan off of a constant, well-planned, master daily-practice schedule. For Thursday, as for any of their practice days, coaches start their practice-planning efforts by working off of a blank master daily-practice schedule, as was detailed in Figure 5-1. One big difference between Thursday's practice schedule and the schedule for both Tuesday and Wednesday is that practice only lasts for one hour and fifteen minutes (i.e., fifteen five-minute practice periods). Furthermore, the last seven periods of practice are devoted to special teams work, as detailed in Figure 9-1.

Planning Thursday's Team-Practice Periods

Figure 9-1 provides an example of an overall base daily-practice plan structure for a light, Thursday, non-padded practice. It should be noted that the schedule does not include any individual or unit drill periods. Since it is Thursday and getting close to game time, the coaching staff, at this point, is totally focused on tuning up the team's overall offensive play.

Date:		Day:		Time:	
Pre-Practice:					
Period	**WR**	**QB**	**RB**	**TE**	**OL**
1	Team Coming-Out Offense vs. Scouts				
2	Team Four Minute Offense vs. Scouts				
3	Team Third-Down Blitz Pick-Up vs. Scouts				
4					
5	Team Red Zone Drive vs. Scouts				
6					
7	Team Two-Minute, Hurry-Hurry Offense vs. Defense				
8					
9	Special Teams Practice				
10					
11					
12					
13					
14					
15					

Figure 9-1. An example of an overall Thursday base practice-plan structure

Coming-out offense, four minute, slow-slow offense, and two-minute, hurry-hurry offense are the final components of the offensive game plan that the team has yet to practice, other than desperation offense and kill-the-clock offense. In addition, many coaches often like to highlight another blitz pick-up period and a brief red zone period that involves having the offense driving to the goal line for a touchdown and a two-point play.

Thursday's practice (period #1) is started with coming-out offense, as detailed in Figure 9-1. This short, five-minute team period must be highly organized and ready to go. It can be helpful when the players know that it is the first drill to be performed on the Thursday practice.

In the drill, the football is usually set six inches from the offense's own goal line, as per the practice script. Initially, the first offense gets a three-play set, followed by a similar set undertaken by the second offense. The drill begins by sending the offense onto the field from the sideline, just as it would in a game-like situation. The offense executes the coming-out drill against the scout squad, as would normally be done during team periods, even though the players are non-padded and only wearing helmets.

Since the schedule only calls for three scripted coming-out offense plays for the first offense and then for the second offense, coaches have two main goals for the five-minute period. In that regard, coaches want to be sure to practice any personnel-substitution plans, as well as formation variations, that are a part of the coming-out offense play call game plan. On occasion, coaches even intentionally send in a play late so that the players who are being substituted for can practice running directly off the field on the sideline through the end zone area, as they are legally allowed to do, rather than scrambling back to the team box area on the 25-yard line. Of course, players who are substituted for can run off the field to their team's sideline, but they can never run off the field through the back endline of the end zone.

Coaches should be sure to practice any of the coming-out offense play calls that are particularly applicable to this extremely important critical game situation. This factor is especially true for plays that the team may not have had the chance to work on to this point of the practice week. For example, they may like to start out with working on a quarterback sneak in an attempt to "punch" the ball out to at least the one-yard line. This scenario is actually a somewhat difficult thing to undertake because of the non-padded aspect of the practice day. On the other hand, coaches make sure that the scout squad players are told beforehand that it's going to be a quarterback sneak, in order to avoid having "submarine"-type action that might stack up bodies and/or result in overly physical play. In reality, the practice mantra of the day for each player is to "exaggerate" his fundaments, even though there is no heavy contact.

During the period devoted to coming-out offense, coaches might practice a very basic run play, such as their inside-zone run play. The reason for doing so might be because they are employing a different personnel plan and/or an alternate formation. As discussed previously, in this relatively brief, five-minute period, coaches want to cover anything—plays, personnel substitutions, or formations—that needs to be addressed in order to be adequately prepared for this critical and, often, extremely dangerous game situation.

Period #2 (as detailed in Figure 9-1) is also a very condensed, tight practice period, one that has a very specific critical, game-situation practice focus—four-minute, slow-slow offense against the scout team. This five-minute period is practiced just as the coming-out offense was in period #1. The first offense executes three plays, and then the second offense goes onto the field to repeat the same set of three practice plays.

The initial practice factor worked on in the drill is for the offense to take every possible second it can off the clock before the football is snapped. As a result, once the offensive huddle is broken, a coach on the field starts counting down (e.g., 12, 11, 10, etc.) in order to allow the quarterback to effectively enact the snap count in a way that utilizes every possible second he can on the clock.

Next, coaches work on outside run-type plays and, possibly even a pass, so that the ballcarrier or receiver can practice staying in-bounds. This point is emphasized so that he doesn't stop the clock from ticking. As was previously discussed in Chapter 8, one exception exists to this rule. If going out of bounds results in gaining first-down yardage, the ballcarrier should definitely do so, since the outcome would convert to a fresh, new set of downs, which would continue to help eat up the clock.

In reality, this practice period should be viewed as a teaching period as much as it is a normal team-practice period. The basic goal of the period is to focus on a critical, game situation, aspect of four-minute, slow-slow offense, which the offense normally doesn't get a lot of opportunity to practice. On one hand, the four minute, slow-slow offense play call game plan provides teams with the ability to engage in additional practice of their best, base, par down run play calls. On the other hand, it is important to remember that it is the mechanics of keeping the clock running and taking as much time off of the clock as possible that are the true focus of this particular five-minute drill.

Periods #3 and #4, as detailed in Figure 9-1, are earmarked for additional work on team blitz pick-up practice. Coaches often, however, tack on third-down practice to the drill to make the exercise a team third-down blitz pick-up drill in order to make the drill as game-like as possible. As a rule, most coaches don't feel that they can ever get enough time to practice blitz pick-up. As such, this drill provides them with one more chance to do so. Given the tendency to be aggressive in blitz pick-up drills, players have to be particularly careful in this drill, because they are not wearing pads. As such, the scout squad and the blockers should be told to perform the drill at a quicker (speed-wise) version of a blitz pick-up, walk-through drill.

Coaches want to be sure that their blockers are not just "tagging off" on the blitz defenders. In fact, coaches want their blockers to *exaggerate* their techniques—whether it is the switching off on a twist or the pick-up of an offside linebacker who is wrapping around a slanting defensive lineman.

Periods #5 and #6, as outlined in Figure 9-1, are devoted to another, although somewhat shorter, team red zone drill. All factors considered, about 14 plays can be squeezed in a 10-minute block of time. On the other hand, the red zone practice repetitions should not be split up between the first and second offense. Rather, all 14 drill practice plays should be executed by the first offense. One step that many coaches take is to substitute key second-team offensive players throughout the drill, whether it is an offensive lineman, tight end, wide receiver, running back, or quarterback. The key focal point is to create a smooth red zone offense tempo on one hand, while taking advantage of an opportunity to practice personnel substitutions and multiple formations, shifts, and motions on the other. As previously noted, red zone offense, for many coaches, includes deep red zone offense, red zone offense, black zone offense, goal line offense, and two-point play offense. As such, coaches should be sure to script up a red zone drive series that includes all of the aforementioned red zone scenarios.

Periods #7 and #8 are assigned to practicing two-minute, hurry-hurry offense, as detailed in Figure 9-1. As the figure indicates, the offense works against the defense. In reality, however, two-minute, hurry-hurry offense can be practiced in a variety of ways, for example, against the defense, against the scout squad, or "on air." Practicing against the defense is a decision undertaken at the discretion of the head coach or the coordinators.

On the other hand, no matter how a team practices its two-minute, hurry-hurry offense, if it works against its own defense, against the scout squad, or "on air," everyone involved must be on the same page with regard to practice tempo. Everyone must be aware that since they are not in pads, they must practice accordingly. This factor is particularly applicable when the offense is working against its own defense, given the competitive nature that typically exists when the offense and defense are working against one another. No one should forget that he is not in pads and that he should not risk being injured by aggressively engaging in practice without the protection by wearing pads.

One excellent way to ensure that a team's offense and defense work against each other on two-minute, hurry-hurry offense and defense, while minimizing the possibility of an injury occurring, is to place some limiting factors on both sides. One option is to have the defensive line and any linebackers or secondary defenders who are attempting to rush the quarterback to take only two or three steps and stop. Simultaneously, the offensive blockers step to their defensive blocking targets, form up their blocks, and then stop. The quarterback and his receivers perform their normal two-minute, hurry-hurry procedures, runs, and pass routes. The defensive secondary reacts to the pass patterns and routes, but allows the receivers to make their catches. The football is moved 10 yards at a time to simulate movement of the football, whether the previous pass was complete or incomplete. As a consequence, teams are able to enact and practice all or, at least, most of the situations attendant to two-minute, hurry-hurry offense—both offensively and defensively. One of the major advantages of this particular format of the team, two-minute, hurry-hurry non-padded exercise is that teams are able to engage in quality practice of the mechanics and communication of this key, critical offensive situation, while at the same time effectively avoiding injuries.

Put Thursday's Play Call Game Plan on Boards in Staff Room

Similar to what they did on Tuesday and Wednesday, coaches put all of their specific coming-out offense , four-minute, slow-slow offense, and two-minute, hurry-hurry play call game plans on the blank play call charts that are positioned on boards in the offensive staff room. In addition, they also record all of these plans in a computer, which allows them to continue to work on completing their actual weekly, game-plan play list.

Creating Thursday's Practice Period Scripts

In fact, creating practice-period scripts for Thursdays is no different than creating practice scripts for Tuesdays and Wednesdays. The dominant practice premise of the day is that the situation is governed by a cut-down mentality, with regard to the length of the practice, as well as the actual number of periods devoted to offensive and defensive practice. The other major factor governing this practice is that it is conducted in a non-padded, non-contact mode and that it uses team-type periods only in the limited amount of practice periods that are available. Coaches still establish a list, or order, of plays that they want to work on in the limited amount time that exists to practice the designated, predetermined, game-like situations. As has been previously discussed, the game-plan play calls have been scripted very specifically for both coming-out offense and four-minute, slow-slow offense, which enables some extremely important critical-situation offense concepts to be addressed that cannot otherwise be covered practicing any other part of the game plan.

The team, third-down, blitz pick-up drill and the team, red zone drive drill are scripted exactly as they were on Tuesday and Wednesday. The only considerations that might vary in this scenario are what other game-plan plays must still be practiced from what other possible personnel plans, formations, shifts, and motions that the coaches are planning to employ. If possible, they try to utilize as many of those types of plays as possible in both of these particular drills on Thursday.

For the team, two-minute, hurry-hurry offense drill, the major consideration is setting up parameters for the actual game-like situation to be practiced. For example, is it that the football is on the offense's own 20-yard line with one minute and 50 seconds left in the game, with the offense having one time-out remaining and needing three points to win the game? Is the football on the offense's own 45-yard line with 50 seconds left in the game, with the offense having two time-outs and needing seven points to win the game? Whatever the situation, the key point to remember is that executing the two-minute, hurry-hurry drill in as game-like a situation as possible, with down-and-distance chain markers and the game clock running, can help both the players and especially the quarterback and coach play caller to practice in an extremely specific and efficient game-like manner.

Scripting Team Scripts

Coaches begin their team scripting efforts in period #1 with a special emphasis team, coming-out offense session. Since this period has a heavy tendency to focus on the use of the run game and, possibly, heavy tight end and H-back use, this particular five-minute scripted period is assigned to the tight end coach, since serving as the coming-out expert tends to have a lot of similarities to the tight end coach being the game-plan expert for goal-line offense and short-yardage offense.

The scripting of four-minute, slow-slow offense in period #2 is designated to the running back coach. As such, serving as the four-minute, slow-slow expert has much in connection with the running back coach, who works directly with the offensive line coach—the team's base, par run-game expert.

For periods #3 and #4 in which a team, third-down blitz pick-up drill is conducted, the 10-minute scripting session is assigned to the offensive line coach, the team's blitz pick-up expert. This designation helps to assure that the offensive players practice their blitz pick-up abilities against the defensive-blitz looks that the offensive line coach feels that they most need to prepare for that week's opponent. The wide receiver coach is given the responsibility of assisting the offensive line coach with the third-down patterns needed for some final, fine-tuning work.

The offensive coordinator scripts the particular team, red zone segment for periods #5 and #6. As a rule, the underlying premise of this assignment is the fact that he usually wants to focus on the offense's extremely critical red zone attack as much as possible for the upcoming opponent. Periods #7 and #8 are devoted to working on two-minute, hurry-hurry offense, which is an otherwise unscripted practice segment. The key concern for this session is getting the hypothetical time, field position, time-outs, and points-needed parameters from the head coach.

10

The Last On-the-Field Practice Review

Hypothetically, it's now early Friday afternoon. The staff has just checked the video from Thursday afternoon's practice. They've analyzed their coming-out offense, their four-minute, slow-slow offense, and their two-minute, hurry-hurry offense to see what they might still need to be added, dropped, or tweaked. They then take a look at their final situational game plans that still require attention—their kill-the-clock offense, their desperation offense, and their last-play offense. At that point, they turn their attention to planning Friday's short, non-padded (including no helmets), tune-up practice.

Kill-the-Clock Offense

Another extremely critical offensive game situation is kill-the-clock offense. Hypothetically, a very limited number of seconds are left on the clock. Your team is ahead on the scoreboard and possesses the football. The opposition does not have enough time-outs to prevent your team from running out the clock. It is time for your critical situation, kill-the-clock offense.

In reality, kill-the-clock offense is actually an extension of a team's four-minute, slow-slow offense. The coaching staff employs a formula to determine whether or not the team can go into its kill-the-clock offense immediately. The other likely possibility is that the team might have to stay in its four-minute, slow-slow offense and gain another first down before it goes into its kill-the-clock offense.

As a rule, most coaches believe that, conservatively, they can run five seconds off the clock on a run play. As such, they might use up more time than five seconds, depending on the speed of the officials in spotting the football and the amount of time the offense can take to unpile from the mass of bodies stacked up on the ballcarrier. Accordingly, coaches can conservatively count on eating up at least 15 seconds of the clock by running the football, even if the defense has three time-outs still available.

As a rule of thumb, coaches can determine whether they can go directly to their kill-the-clock offense or they have to remain in their four-minute, slow-slow offense and gain another first down by adding 40 seconds of running time for every time-out the defense does not have. Realistically, coaches can also count on using up another five seconds on a fourth-down run play if necessary, in order to run out a last few seconds to win the game. Figure 10-1 provides an example of a four-minute, slow-slow offense or kill-the-clock calculation chart.

Four-Minute, Slow-Slow or Kill-The-Clock Offense Conversion Chart

(3) Time-outs – 15 seconds

(2) Time-outs – 55 seconds

(1) Time-out – 1:35

(0) Time-outs – 2:15

Figure 10-1. An example of a four-minute, slow-slow or kill-the-clock conversion chart

More often than not, a kill-the-clock offense uses two basic formations, depending on which of the three basic kill-the clock offense plays that the offense will employ. Figure 10-2 illustrates an example of a typical kill-the-clock offense formation. It should be noted that this basic kill-the-clock formation includes two close-to-the-line-of-scrimmage blockers and a super-deep tail back, who is aligned 11 yards deep to act as a baseball-type shortstop, just in case anything goes wrong with the snap and/or the quarterback's possession of the football.

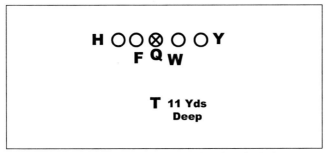

Figure 10-2. An example of a basic kill-the-clock formation

From this basic, kill-the-clock formation, several plays can be run. Two of the most commonly employed plays in this situation are kill-take-a-knee and kill-stay-alive. In kill-take-a-knee, the quarterback takes the snap, takes a knee, and then quickly runs to the official who is behind him to give him the football. On kill-stay-alive, the quarterback takes the snap, steps back a yard and a half, and then sits in that blocked pocket (formed by offensive linemen and up-positioned blockers) for as long as he can. Executing this step enables the quarterback to eat up a few, additionally needed, extra seconds off the clock. Subsequently, once the quarterback starts to feel defensive-rush pressure, he takes a knee and flops over to his side, curled around the football. The up-blockers then cover the quarterback by actually laying on him in layers, which can help to run off another few, precious seconds off the clock, given that the players who are lying on the quarterback will have to get off the quarterback at some point, layer by layer.

On the kill-take-a-safety play, the players align in a slightly different arrangement. The two up-backs become wingbacks to help guard against fast, outside pressure on the quarterback as he engages in his take-a-safety action. In addition, the super-deep tailback reduces his depth down to seven yards deep, positioned to the left (for a right handed quarterback), while stacking over the tackle. His initial goal is to clear a path for the quarterback's dropback action.

Once the quarterback passes the tailback, the tailback steps back to the center's midline to become an extra personal protector for the quarterback, as the quarterback works his take-a-safety action. On the kill-take-a-safety play, the quarterback sprints to an area approximately one yard from the back of the endline of the end zone. From that point, he can work laterally to the right or left if he can to avoid any defensive-rush pressure in order to eat up additional time, before *sprinting* out-of-bounds across the back endline or even the sideline of the end zone. Sprinting out-of-bounds can help the quarterback avoid a possible big hit from a defender. The kill-take-a-safety formation and play are illustrated in Figure 10-3.

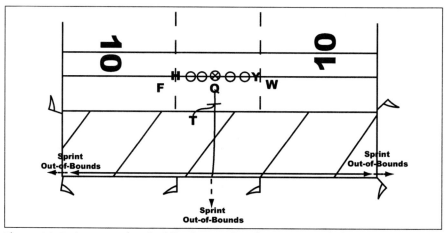

Figure 10-3. An example of a kill-take-a-safety formation and play

Creating a Kill-the-Clock Play Call Game Plan

As has been previously discussed, most teams have three plays that are on their kill-the-clock offense game-plan, play call list that tends to stay constant for each week of the season. In the example that is detailed in Figure 10-4, the three plays are kill, kill-stay-alive, and kill-take-a-safety.

KILL OFFENSE

KILL
KILL-STAY-ALIVE
KILL-TAKE-A-SAFETY

Figure 10-4. An example of a kill-the-clock offense game-plan, play call list

Desperation Offense

For most teams, their desperation offense entails a single play—the "Hail Mary." The term "Hail Mary" encompasses a formation call, a blocking call, and a pass-pattern call all-in-one. An example of the "desperation" formation and "Hail Mary" play call is illustrated in Figure 10-5.

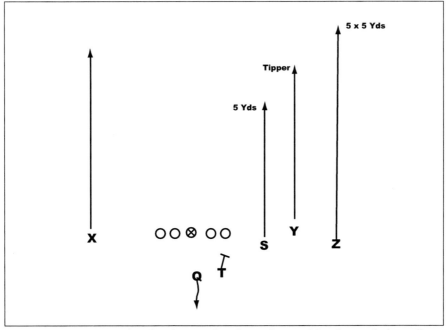

Figure 10-5. An example of a desperation formation and "Hail Mary" play call

On the desperation play shown, the players align in a three-by-one spread trips formation. The offense continues to employ a four-wide receiver personnel structure. The backside, single receiver runs a streak route. If the quarterback has a reasonably good opportunity to hit a one-on-one streak isolation route to the backside, he should take it. Otherwise, the quarterback should work the desperation portion of the pattern, as detailed in Figure 10-6. When throwing to the desperation portion of the pattern, the quarterback should launch a high, lofty pass that should purposely die over the top of the middle receiver—the "tipper." The tipper can either tip the football back to the inside, trailing receiver or outside and behind himself to the deep, outside receiver. Of course, the tipper should always try to catch the ball if he is in the end zone. As a rule, the tipper is normally a taller receiver, who has good jumping ability.

Teams can also include a special, trick play or a second desperation offense play as part of their desperation-play package. For example, Figure 10-6 provides an example of a deep, square-out desperation pass that could be employed in an effort to get a deep chunk of pass yardage for a field goal try. It should also be noted that the receiver must remember to get the ball out-of-bounds to stop the clock after he catches the pass. An example of a desperation offense game-plan, play call list is detailed in Figure 10-7.

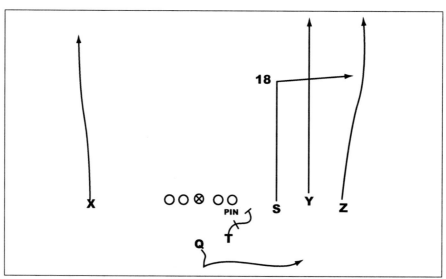

Figure 10-6. An example of a deep, square-out desperation pass

DESPERATION OFFENSE	
DESPERATION RT	DESPERATION LT
DESPERATION RT SLOT SQUARE-OUT	DESPERATION LT SLOT SQUARE-OUT

Figure 10-7. An example of a desperation offense game-plan, play call list

Last-Play Sequence

For many teams, their last-play sequence is a part of their desperation offense. For example, if teams were to complete their desperation play and found themselves within striking distance of the end zone, with very few seconds left on the clock and had no time-outs remaining, they want to be sure to have a system in place to efficiently get a sound play called and executed. Similarly, if teams were running out the clock for halftime and popped a trap for 50 yards to the opponent's 12-yard line, for example, and two seconds were left on the clock, they need to be well-practiced and well-prepared to execute one last play before the game time left in the first half expires.

The underlying theory of the last-play sequence is that if a scenario arises in which a team has a successful long play that produces a first down but has no time-outs remaining, it will "clock" the football by throwing a quick pass to the ground, if, at least, four are left on the clock. This situation would give the offense an opportunity to run one last play or kick a field goal attempt. If there are three seconds or less are left on the clock, teams shouldn't *trust* the clock. As a result, they will not "clock" the football. Instead, the quarterback will call a predetermined, memorized play from his team's constant last-play sequence play call ready list, which hopefully will allow him to throw a pass into the end zone for a chance to score. On the other hand, if his team was inside the two-yard line, the quarterback could call for a run play.

The basic reasoning underlining the quarterback's last play sequence play calling is that if the football is outside the opponent's 20-yard line, the quarterback should know to call some type of four-vertical or four-deep pass pattern. From the plus 20- to the plus 10-yard lines, another type of last play sequence pass pattern would be on the ready list for the quarterback to call. The play called would, again, probably be some type of play call that if and when the ball was caught, the receiver would be able to score a touchdown because of his positioning in the end zone. From the nine-yard line to the two, teams would probably employ pass plays that are from their quick-pass or five-step drop-pass game that would lead to a touchdown once the ball was caught, such as a fade or square-in route. Another possibility would be to utilize a route combination, such as a slant, which would allow the receiver to either catch the football in the end zone for a touchdown or run the football into the end zone for a touchdown. When his team is on the two- or one-yard line, the quarterback has the choice of either making a quick-pass call or running the football with a run or run-option play.

Creating a Last-Play Sequence Play Call Game Plan

As has previously been noted, teams that have a set last-play sequence play call game plan will often employ that plan for the entire season. Memorized and well-practiced, the quarterback knows he is responsible to call a last play if the situation is the end of the half or the game, no time outs are remaining, and three seconds or less are left on the clock. Figure 10-8 outlines an example of a last-play sequence, game-plan, play call list. For all teams who might find themselves in such a situation, the goal is to be well-practiced and fully ready to execute a solid play that would enable them to get the football in the end zone and score a touchdown.

Last-Play Sequence Play Call List

+20 or Deeper: 4 vertical routes pattern or some type of deep 3- or 4-route pattern combination

+19 to +10:   Scissors—a hi/lo smash pattern to one side with a deep post/flag route combination to the other

+9 to +3:   Double slants to the slot side and a slant/flat route combination to the flanker/tight end side

+2 to +1:   Quarterback's choice of inside zone, speed option, or any applicable quick pass

---

Figure 10-8. An example of a last-play sequence, game-plan, play call list

11

Practice Planning Friday's Play Call Game Plans

Friday is the last true practice session of the week. It is an extremely short session, typically lasting only 45 minutes. The last 15 minutes are concerned with special team's substitutions. The players do not wear pads or helmets. The offense does not work against the scout squad. All practice work is team-oriented with plays for run against "air." Practice work is conducted in a team's own stadium if it's a home game or if the team has the time to do so before it has to travel. Teams will practice in their opponent's stadium when they're on the road if they can't practice at home before they depart for travel.

Teams generally have two offensive practice goals on Friday. The first goal is to go through a full red zone offense drive. It may be worthwhile to extend the red zone drive sequence a few extra plays to allow for the practice of a special play that might need extra practice or a key third down play that may require a special personnel plan substitution or just needs extra practice attention.

The Friday red zone practice sequence starts with two deep red zone passes, one from the plus 40 yard line going in and one from the 35 yard line. The next two play practice repetitions accommodate the need for the practice of that key special play or third down play. Ball placement for those plays would probably be on the 30 and 25 yard lines to produce the momentum of entering the red zone. The next eight plays would constitute two four play down series (first, second, third, and fourth downs) as the offense works from the 20 yard line to the goal line. No specific number of red zone plays, black zone plays, or goal line plays is set. That determination is up to the offensive coordinator, so that he can place emphasis on plays he feels need the most last minute practice attention.

The total, slightly extended red zone drive, culminated in the practice play of two, two-point plays comes to 14 play repetitions. Only run the first offense for such a practice, but be sure to make key substitution needs throughout the drill. The chains and down markers are used and the red zone area is carefully marked off (usually with cones). Friday's practice also includes a heavy dose of working on utilizing varied personnel, formation, shifts, and motions during the extended red zone drive. All of these factors can be key determinants in how well the offense functions, along with the large amount of substitution practice.

The second goal that many coaches have for their Friday's practice is to work on their kill-the-clock offense, their desperation offense, and their last-play sequence offense. Once they finish practicing those aspects, they will have covered every critical offensive-game situation that they might face, come game time in their effort to win.

Planning Off of a Daily Master Practice Plan

Just as has been done all week for the planning of Tuesday through Thursday's practices, the key to sound practice planning for Friday is to plan off of a constant, well-planned, master daily-practice schedule. On Friday, similar to any of the practice days, coaches start their practice-planning efforts by working off of a blank master daily-practice schedule, as was detailed in Figure 5-1, in Chapter 5. As they did on Thursday, coaches typically shorten Friday's session, practicing for 45 minutes only (i.e., nine five-minute practice periods). In addition, the last three periods of practice are devoted to practicing special teams substitution, as illustrated in Figure 11-1.

Planning Friday's Team-Practice Periods

Figure 11-1 provides an example of an overall base daily-practice plan structure for a light, non-padded, non-helmeted practice. It should be noted that Friday's practice does not include any individual or unit drill periods. Given that it is Friday and getting close to game time, coaches are totally focused on continuing on the effort to tune up their team's overall offensive play. Kill-the clock offense, desperation offense, and last-play sequence offense are the last components of their offensive game plan that they have yet to practice. The Friday practice schedule also includes another slightly elongated, red zone period, involving driving to the goal line for a touchdown and a two-point play try. All of the practice work for the day is team-period work and is run "on air," rather than against a scout squad. The practice focuses for Friday are timing, personnel substitutions, and working on varied formations, shifts, and motions.

Date:		Day:		Time:	
Pre-Practice:					
Period	**WR**	**QB**	**RB**	**TE**	**OL**
1					
2		Team Red Zone Drive vs. Air			
3					
4		Team Desperation Offense vs. Air			
5		Team Last-Play Sequence vs. Air			
6		Team Kill-the-Clock Offense vs. Air			
7					
8		Special Teams Substitution Practice			
9					

Figure 11-1. An example of an overall Friday base practice-plan structure

Friday's practice (periods #1 to #3) is started with a slightly elongated, red zone offense drive. In this instance, elongated refers to the fact that a four-play series from the 30-yard line is added, after two deep red zone pass-play repetitions. Such practicing can help teams concentrate on, what most coaches feel, is one of the three most critical game situations that they will face in the game. As noted previously, another factor that coaches also like about practicing a full red zone drive on Fridays, with its added four-play series from the 30-yard line, is that it allows them to also address the two other critical game situations that can be very important to whether the offense will be successful—base, par down offense and third-down offense. It should be noted that only the first offense is involved in this segment of practice. As was stated previously, teams practice their personnel plan substitutions and key player substitutions heavily at this time, utilizing a significant number of their offensive players.

Period #4 is devoted to practicing desperation offense. In this session, a team may start on the 50-yard line, for example, in order to be able to easily flow into its next period's targeted focus—the last-play sequence offense. Coaches want to make sure that they are sound with their ability to insert any special desperation offense personnel they might want in the line-up. On occasion, they might also make a deep one-on-one streak throw to their lone receiver, who is positioned away from the trips side. In addition, they often move the football up closer to the goal line so that any desperation pass that is thrown definitely winds up in the end zone. This step helps the "tipper" to understand that if he can jump up and make a catch in the end zone, his team will score six points. He needs to be aware that his priority is to catch the pass when in the end zone. He does not need to tip the ball forwards or backwards to one of the two other receivers if he, himself, can make the touchdown catch. Teams also practice any supplemental or special, trick desperation plays that they may want to be game-ready for that week's opponent at this time.

Period #5 is assigned to practicing the team's last-play sequence. Hypothetically, the offense has just produced a big play or at least gained a first down and has just enough time (a mere few seconds), with no time-outs remaining, to get off one last play. As a rule, it is most facilitating to tack on the working of the last-play sequence offense to the last practice repetition of desperation offense from the previous period.

For example, a coach might call out the following hypothetical situation—"caught for a first down, there are three seconds in the game, and the offense has no time-outs." At this point, the quarterback must take over and call a memorized play from his last-play sequence offense play call ready list, a decision that is affected by the yardage and hash consideration concerning where the football is placed.

In order to practice dealing with the aforementioned situation, the coaching staff can have the offense cope with several variations of that particular set of circumstances. For example, on the first repetition, the football could be placed on, or beyond, the plus 20-yard line. The second repetition could involve positioning the football somewhere between the plus 19 and the plus 10-yard line, which in turn could lead to a call by the coach in which he is trying to set a specific field situation, e.g., "first down on the 12-yard line, one second left on the clock, no time-outs." The third repetition could entail a football placement of somewhere between the nine-yard and the three-yard line. The fourth and final repetition could see the football being placed on either the two-yard or the one-yard line. In each situation, the quarterback must take command of the situation. No coach wants, amidst all of the excitement and possible disarray on the sideline, to be in a situation where his quarterback has to locate the play call signaler on the sideline with only a second or two left in the game.

In reality, coaches often like to incorporate a fifth repetition somewhere amidst the four previously discussed last-play sequence offense calls. As such, on one of the repetitions, the facilitating coach will call out a situation as he is placing the football, but states that "four" seconds are left on the clock. With four seconds or more left on the clock, the quarterback can call for a "clock" play, one in which he spikes the football to the ground after receiving the snap from the center. On any repetition in which this is done, the facilitating coach simply picks up from where he left off to be sure to expedite all five of the last-play sequence offense play call situations.

Period #6 is devoted to working on a team's kill-the-clock offense series, which it does immediately after practicing its last-play sequence offense. In this situation, the coaching staff turns the offense around and positions the football on the minus five-yard line. This step is designed to help a team efficiently practice its kill-take-a-safety play, one of the plays on the kill-the-clock play call ready list of most teams. It also forces a team's kill offense to be extremely careful if it is executing its kill-stay-alive play. The quarterback *must* be sure that he is not taking a knee on, or behind, the goal line.

Most coaches also like the idea of working on substituting players deep in their own territory, since any substitution mistake made this deep in their own territory could prove extremely costly.

The last, actual, on-the-field practice repetition for most teams, after a week's long preparation, involves working on their kill-take-a-knee play. All factors considered, this offensive play call is the best play a coach can ever make.

Put Friday's Play Call Game Plan on Boards in the Staff Room

Just as they did on the previous three days (Tuesday through Thursday), coaches make sure to add any game-plan play calls to the play call boards in their staff room. More often than not, however, a team's desperation offense, last-play call offense, and kill-the-clock offense are, for the most part, fixed plans that coaches use all season long, from game to game. As a result, these plans are already on the boards. As such, all coaches need to do is to add any supplementary, special, or trick plays to the game plan for all three of these critical-offense situations. In addition, at this point, coaches also input all of their possible additions into their computer, in order to continue their progress on completing their actual weekly game-plan play list.

Creating Friday's Practice-Period Scripts

Creating a practice-period script for Fridays is no different than creating practice scripts for Tuesday through Thursday. The dominant, underlying practice premise for the day is that coaches want to reduce both the length of practice and the actual number of periods devoted to offensive and defensive practice. The other key practice parameter is that practice is conducted in a non-padded, non-contact mode, without wearing helmets. Furthermore, Friday's practice only employs team-type periods in the limited amount of practice periods in which the team has to work. A list (i.e., order) of plays that the coaching staff wants to work on in the limited amount of available practice time targets predetermined, game-like situations.

On Fridays, however, the only periods that tend to be scripted are the first three, which are devoted to a slightly elongated team, red zone drive. A team's desperation offense, last-play sequence offense, and kill-the-clock offense are all listed on its play call sheets for the year, since it normally employs them from game to game. As a result, the only factor that coaches might want to work on during the specific practice period is a new, supplementary play or a special, trick play.

Scripting Team Scripts

As noted previously, the only team periods on Friday that have to be scripted are periods #1 through #3, which are used for an elongated, red zone drive. This drive involves a variety of offensive focuses, including deep red zone, red zone, black zone goal line, and two-point play offense. Coaches may choose to extend this specific red zone drive to include an extra, four-play series, starting at the 30-yard line.

The underlying focus of the team, red zone drive exercise is twofold. Initially, coaches want to be sure to work on any plays in the game plan that might still need attention or "touching up" in practice. Coaches also want to practice any game-plan play call that, for whatever reason, has still not been practiced, such as a reverse or a base run play from a formation that has not already been practiced that week.

The other key focus of the team, red zone drive is, quite simply, to help promote a clear-cut, efficient sense of a confident, dominant playing tempo. This occasion is not the time to create misunderstanding or confusion in the offense. Because the offense needs to finish this practice confidently and ready to go, the offensive coordinator usually scripts the team, red zone drive exercise.

Friday Night Offensive Meeting

On Friday night, the evening before the upcoming game, the offensive staff has a half-hour to 45-minute meeting. This gathering gives the offensive coordinator an opportunity to talk about the game and reiterate his key concerns. As a rule, at this time, many teams review their play call reasoning and concepts for the game's first two series, in order to help produce both a focus on and a comfort zone with what the players should expect to be called early in the game. This interplay allows the players to check with their position coaches if they have any last-minute questions.

Coaches finish the Friday night meeting by watching a premade video of the defense of the next day's opponent. The video shows the defensive fronts and coverages that can be expected against examples of offensive formations and personnel plans that are similar to the type of plays that the offense anticipates utilizing.

The Hay Is in the Barn When …

As the physical intensity that occurs during the week of practice gradually lessens in an effort to allow the players to get refreshed and more rested come game time, most coaches work hard to pick up on the mental, assignment aspects of the game. One statement that no coach wants to hear after the last, truly physical practice on Wednesday is "the hay is in the barn!" While coaches may cut back on the physical aspects of practice as the week progresses, they more than make up for the reduction in the level of physical demands that occur during practice with a heightened focus on the mental aspects of the game, as their team gets closer and closer to kick-off time. The key point to remember is that every coach and every player must fully understand that "the hay is in the barn" *just prior to the football being kicked off come game time and not a second sooner.*

12

Game-Day Preparation

It's game day, and kick-off is only a handful of hours away. At this point, many coaches might feel that "the hay is now truly in the barn." In reality, they're mistaken. Plenty of time is left for a pregame walk-through.

Pregame Walk-Through

Twenty minutes before breakfast or their pre-game meal, many teams conduct one, final walk-through exercise. The walk-through involves 15 minutes, which gives the players and coaching staff five minutes to be on time for the team meal. Whether the players are still waking up or, perhaps, a bit lethargic from sitting around their hotel room for an extended period of time, a short walk-through session can help to get the players' blood flowing and their minds refocused on the game and their assignments.

For this final walk-through exercise, the offensive coordinator and the offensive line coach create the script, which includes both plays they want the team to work on and defenses that they anticipate facing. The script includes 12 to 15 plays. At this point, coaches focus on two factors. First, they want to review any plays (run or pass) that have given the team particular problems during the course of the practice week when executed against specific defensive looks. Second they try to work on additional blitz pick-up practice, focusing on the blitzes that seem to have given the offense the most problems during the course of the practice week.

And then, at this point, the team is ready to go. The offense is well-prepared. The coaches feel confident that they have covered every base and then some. Kick-off is just around the corner. *It's time to go and win!*

About the Author

Steve Axman was most recently the assistant head coach and offensive coordinator at the University of Idaho. Prior to that, he was the wide receivers coach at the University of Washington, a position he assumed before the 2004 season. It was Axman's second stint on the Huskies staff. Previously, he served as the assistant head coach and quarterbacks coach. Axman oversaw the work of UW record-setting quarterbacks Marques Tuiasosopo and Cody Pickett. During the 2003 season, he was the offensive coordinator and quarterbacks coach at UCLA.

Axman is no stranger to wide-open, multiple offense football or producing top-flight collegiate quarterbacks. During his career, he has worked at four Pac-10 schools (UCLA, Arizona, Stanford, and Washington). Among his former collegiate pupils are Troy Aikman and Drew Olsen (UCLA), Neil O'Donnell (Maryland), and Jeff Lewis and Travis Brown (Northern Arizona).

In 1998 (prior to joining the UW staff the first time), Axman served as the quarterbacks coach at Minnesota under Glen Mason. Before that, Axman was the head coach at Northern Arizona from 1990-97. He inherited a NAU program that had experienced just three winning seasons during the 1980s and had never qualified for the Division I-AA postseason playoffs. During his eight years with the Lumberjacks, Axman guided the team to a 48-41 record, making him the second-winningest coach in Northern Arizona's history.

Axman's NAU teams were known for their offensive fireworks. During his eight-year career, Axman's teams averaged 30 points per game. His 1996 Lumberjack squad set or tied 14 national records and averaged 43.2 points per game en route to a 9-3 overall record and a 6-1 record in the Big Sky Conference. That season produced a second-place finish in the Big Sky, the school's first postseason appearance, and a school-best No. 6 national ranking. In 1989, Axman served as quarterbacks coach for Maryland, where he worked with O'Donnell. In 1987-88, he was the offensive coordinator at UCLA, where he coached Aikman. Prior to UCLA, Axman coached at Stanford (1986), with the Denver Gold of the United States Football League (1985), and at the University of Arizona (1980-1984), as the offensive coordinator and quarterbacks coach. Axman previously spent a year at Illinois, three seasons at Army, and one season at Albany State. Prior to that, Axman's first collegiate coaching assignment was at East Stroudsburg State in 1974. A 1969 graduate of C.W. Post College in Greenvale, NY, Axman went on to earn his first master's degree from Long Island University in 1972 and his second in 1975 while coaching at East Stroudsburg State College.

Axman has authored 11 instructional books on football. He has also been featured on seven well-received instructional videos on football. He is nationally renowned for his knowledge of offensive fundamentals, schemes, and techniques, particularly quarterback play.

A native of Huntington Station, NY, Axman and his wife, Dr. Marie Axman, an elementary school principal, have four daughters: Mary Beth, Jaclyn, Melissa, and Kimberly.

Books by Steve Axman

- 101 Concepts for Effective Football Practice
- Attacking Coverages With the Passing Game
- Coaching Critical Situation Offense
- Coaching Quarterback Passing Mechanics (Second Edition)
- Coaching the Offensive Backs (Third Edition)
- 101 Concepts for Effective Offense
- 101 Pass Dropback Patterns
- 101 Quarterback Drills
- The Complete Handbook of Offensive Football Drills
- Attacking Modern Defenses With a Multiple Formation Veer Offense
- The Pro-Read Option Attack for Winning Football